USING THE BIBLE IN EVANGELISM

DEREK TIDBALL

BIBLE SOCIETY

British and Foreign Bible Society
Stonehill Green, Westlea, Swindon, SN5 7DG, England

© Derek Tidball 1985, 1993

First published 1985. Revised edition 1993

All quotations from the Bible are from the Good News Bible,
published by the Bible Societies/HarperCollins © American Bible
Society, New York, 1966, 1971 and 4th edition 1976.

ISBN 0-564-084557

Cover Design by Jane Taylor
Printed and bound in Great Britain by Biddles Ltd, Guildford

CONTENTS

TO BEGIN WITH...

Colin read in the *Reader's Digest* that the two longest books in the world were the *Bible* and *War and Peace*. He decided he wanted to read both of them. Knowing nothing of the Bible he naturally began at the beginning but found it hard going. When he got as far as Leviticus a Christian he knew came to his rescue and offered to study it with him. He agreed, providing they began where he had left off. They did, and Colin soon became overwhelmed with the holiness of God and the need for his sins to be forgiven. He quickly learned that Jesus was "the Lamb of God, who takes away the sin of the world" (John 1.29).

Julian went on a student trip to see Jesus Christ Superstar and that got him thinking about Jesus. So he went to a bookshop and looked around for something which didn't appear too "churchy." He bought a *Good News New Testament,* went home to read it, and found he couldn't stop. He read it right through, and as he read each page his world seemed to change, and Jesus became real to him. He didn't know any Christians and it was six months before he started going to church regularly. The Bible alone had been instrumental in his conversion.

Frank was an embittered prisoner in Dartmoor who rudely rejected every attempt the Chaplain made to help him. That was until his mother died. Attending the funeral, he was given her New Testament and began reading it on the way back to jail. Upon his return he asked to see the prison Chaplain and became a Christian.

Alan's mother had read Greek at university and out of interest she acquired a Greek New Testament from Bible Society. Though not an ardent believer herself, she kept in touch with the Society and years later they sent her a free copy of Good News told by Luke. She threw it away, but Alan was thinking about religion at the time and fished it out of the dustbin. He was not sure that it was actually part of the Bible, but nonetheless it introduced him to the life of Jesus in a new way. A few weeks later, at a gospel concert, he was converted.

John was a strict Moslem, who had been steeped in the Koran from his birth. His reading of the gospel led to his conversion to Christianity and eventually to his becoming a bishop in India.

Ken was gripped with fear about the future of the world. He was so riddled with anxiety that if he read the newspaper before going to work it finished him — he couldn't face the world that day. One winter's evening he had been visited by the Jehovah's Witnesses and they had fuelled his neurosis. A week later, a member of the parish church called at his house as part of a town-wide Scripture distribution programme and left him an extract from Matthew. Within a week Ken became a Christian and the fear gradually melted away, not least because of the teaching of the Sermon on the Mount which he had originally been given.

The Bible is one of the most effective evangelistic tools we have. These accounts of people who have come to faith because of it represent countless numbers who have found faith because someone gave them a Bible at school; left one in a hospital, prison, or hotel; invited them to a Bible study group; or engaged in evangelistic visiting. They came from all sorts of backgrounds. Some, like Kriss Akabusi, the athlete, are well-known. Most are unknown.

One of our urgent needs in evangelism today is to rediscover a confidence in the Bible. It has received so many knocks in the classroom, from the media, and from the pulpit, that many Christians have lost confidence in it. But those challenges can be countered, and if our confidence can be restored, so that we do use the Bible in evangelism, we might be surprised at the results.

This book is written in the firm conviction that it is possible to use the Bible in evangelism even in our "post-Christian society." More than that, it is written in the conviction that our failure to use the Bible is the cause of much of our ineffectiveness.

The Bible is one of the great untapped resources of the evangelistic work of the church. Our attitude to it reminds me of a newspaper cutting I saw about the coming of electricity to the Isle of Skye. A reporter had asked an old crofter what difference the electricity had made to his life. "Och," he replied, "it's great! It means that every evening I can switch on the light and see to light my oil lamp, then I switch it off again." We enjoy struggling in the dim light of our own words and methods when God has already made available a brilliant resource which we ignore.

Recent momentous changes in our world scene gives us new opportunities to see the Bible at work, if we will seize them. Doors have opened in Eastern Europe which none could have envisaged a few years back. To meet the opportunity the United Bible Societies plan to provide 30 million scriptures. At home, in the post-Thatcher years when people's economic and technological dreams have failed, there is a new openness to spiritual answers.

A.M.Chirgwin, in his study *The Bible in World Evangelism,* wrote

> *Throughout its history the Christian Church has used the Bible as a main instrument of its evangelistic activity... This evidence of history is impressive... the times when the Church has gone to its evangelistic task with the Bible open in its hands have been precisely the times when it has won many of its greatest conquests. The Bible has in fact been the cutting-edge of its advance.*

Later he commented,

> *It has proved its ability to speak to men of every condition, country and culture. It is the weapon par excellence of the Church's warfare which, if well wielded, may have a large part in winning the world for Christ.*

I became aware personally how effective the Bible was in communicating with non-Christians some years ago, when engaged in "coffee bar evangelism". I was chatting to a group of ordinary and not very Christian teenagers. They were talking of the difficulties they found in doing what was right and the draw they felt towards wrong, even when they wanted to do right. After the conversation had been going on for some time I took out my New Testament and read to them from Romans 7.15–20. They reacted as if they had been caught red-handed. They had no idea that the Bible understood them, nor that it could describe their situation so exactly. Those verses did not immediately lead to their conversion, but they lent credibility to the Bible and opened the way for them to listen further to the news about Jesus. Since then I have been persuaded that the Bible is too important to be kept locked up in the Church.

Using the Bible in evangelism does not mean that it will always play the same part in the evangelistic process. It may be the sole means of conversion, or it may just arouse someone's interest or secure their response. Nor does it mean that we have to adopt some narrow or particular evangelistic method. It allows us to use a wide variety of approaches. It is the aim of this book to indicate some of that variety. We begin by discussing evangelism and the way the early Christians used the Scriptures. We look at the Good News which they shared. After that we discuss some of the problems of using the Bible today and lay some ground rules for that use. The final chapters of the book suggest practical ways in which the Bible can be used in different circumstances.

The great Victorian preacher, C.H. Spurgeon, once said, "Defend the Bible! I'd rather defend a lion. Release it and let it go and it will defend itself." In the same spirit the purpose of this book is not to present an academic discussion, but practical guidelines which will enable the Bible to be released, so it can do the work for which God intended it.

1. SHARING GOOD NEWS TODAY

WHAT IS EVANGELISM?

Philip, the early church evangelist, was called away by the Holy Spirit from his evangelistic work in Samaria to talk with one man who was on his way home from Jerusalem to Ethiopia. When they met, Philip "told him the Good News about Jesus" (Acts 8.35). In a nutshell, that is evangelism. It is to share the Good News about Jesus.

Naturally there are many questions which arise from such a simple statement but, for the moment, let us note three aspects of our simple definition.

It is news about Jesus

Evangelism concerns a message about Jesus Christ. We might well talk about our church or our opinions as we envangelize, but unless we talk in some way about Jesus we cannot claim to be evangelizing. The early Christians had almost only one topic of conversation — what they believed God had done in the life, teaching, death, and resurrection of Jesus of Nazareth, and what they believed he was going to do when Jesus returned. We shall discuss this more fully in Chapter 3 on p 26.

It is news which is good

The Good News is that "God did not send his son into the world to be its judge, but to be its saviour" (John 3.17). Most people in the world are only too well aware of its problems and the power of evil, even if many refuse to accept any responsibility for what happens. They have enough people offering condemnation and adding to their burdens. They have enough moralists offering apparent solutions. But in Jesus there is news, which many have not heard, and which is the real solution.

It is news to be shared

Most of us find it difficult to keep good news to ourselves. If something happens to us which we find exciting, we let it bubble over in our conversations and others soon get the message. I was out of range of the news media for most of the time the abortive coup took place against Gorbachov, and particularly during the hours when the coup collapsed and he was restored to power. I was travelling across Europe on public transport. But by the time I reached home that night I had been told the news several times over. You cannot keep good news quiet.

So it should be with the Good News about Jesus. The responsibility for sharing that news does not lie with church leaders alone, nor with any specialist group, but with every Christian. Nor should it be thought that the Good News has to be shared in a particular way. It does not, as will become evident later. To this we might add two other preliminary comments.

It is usually a process

Sometimes one hears of Christians who are able to meet another person for the first time and within a few minutes share Jesus with them so completely that the person becomes a Christian. But that is rare, and even when it appears, as in the case of Philip and the Ethiopian official, the person who responds so immediately has usually been thinking deeply about the issues beforehand.

Most of the time evangelism is a sort of process, and we only act in part of that process. Recent research suggests the process of finding faith takes an average of four years. There is no single chain of events that everyone goes through, but there are often common features. Often a person follows Jesus because of the positive impression made on them by family or friends who already believe. Sometimes it begins because a person faces a particular problem, either in themselves or their circumstances. Just at that time the person's interest in Christian things may somehow be aroused. If they like the package in which the Good News is presented to them they may be encouraged to inquire further. Then they may come to appreciate more the relevance of the Christian message for their life. The turning point comes when they respond positively to the Good News and become a Christian.

James F. Engel has developed a model which clarifies what is involved in evangelism and helps to show what we ought to be aiming for as we seek to share the Good News. Here is an adaptation of the Engel scale, showing the stages a person may go through as they come to faith.

-10 Awareness of the supernatural
-9 No effective knowledge of Christianity
-8 Initial awareness of Christianity
-7 Interest in Christianity
-6 Awareness of the basic facts of the gospel
-5 Grasp of implications of the gospel
-4 Positive attitude to the gospel
-3 Awareness of personal need
-2 Challenge and decision to act
-1 Repentance and faith
                              A guide to the process of evangelism
                                      Adapted from the Engel Scale

Becoming a Christian is only a turning point. The process of evangelism is not completed until the person becomes a member of the church, fully accepting their responsibilities as a member of the family of God and a disciple of Jesus Christ, and sharing the Good News with others.

Whether we are involved in the whole process or just a tiny part of it, we should keep clearly in mind that the essence of evangelism is sharing the Good News about Jesus.

Evangelism has both a narrow and a broad focus

Our definition of evangelism emphasizes the narrow focus. We have been looking at evangelism through a zoom lens, as it were, and have seen it close up. But it is also important that we use a wide-angle lens to see it in its broader setting. If we switch lenses two other aspects of the same picture become apparent.

1. Although we have spoken of the Good News as if it were exclusively for individuals, it is also for society. Jesus said that God was breaking into human history and inaugurating a new reign, usually known as the Kingdom of God. That kingdom has widespread social implications. In the same way, when individuals turn to God they must turn away from their sin, something which again has social as well as personal implications.

2. We will often share the Good News in what we say, but the broader focus helps us to see that other means of communication are also important. The New Testament writers stressed the significance of living holy lives as a means of showing Jesus to

others. They announced the Good News of Jesus by miracles and healings. These were dramatic demonstrations of the words they had spoken and they lent authority to their claims about Jesus. It is foolish to drive a wedge between visual and verbal ways of sharing the Good News. Word, works and wonders all belong together. However, it must be said that, in the end, it is necessary to share the Good News verbally, to make sure that the message is communicated clearly and is fully understood.

The broader focus on evangelism has sometimes led people into a side-track where the social actions, the miracles, or whatever it may be takes over becoming ends in themselves and considered to be the sum total of evangelism. Important though these things may be, it is even more important not to lose sight of the narrow focus of evangelism if we are to be effective evangelists.

"3-P" EVANGELISM

Another helpful way of looking at evangelism is to distinguish three aspects of the evangelistic task. All of them are important in their own right, but none of them can afford to stand alone.

Evangelism as presence

From the beginning, evangelism included not only words but works. This can be seen in the ministry of Jesus. His preaching was built on the foundation of the incarnation and the miracles and good deeds he performed. We need to be involved in Christian action today, otherwise whatever we say will have little effect and be less than complete obedience to our Lord, who called us to be salt as well as light.

Action is important

The work of a woman like Mother Teresa of Calcutta shows what an impact can be made by the witness of works. Christian service builds bridges to people who do not follow Jesus Christ and establishes a position from which we can talk about him, as well as being right for its own sake.

This makes it essential that Christians do not remain in any sort of clique. It is tempting to stay within the secure boundaries of the Christian community and to retreat into it whenever life permits. Belief in God then becomes a matter of maximum personal enjoyment but of minimum social relevance, and we keep our private and our public worlds wide apart.

The result of this is that when we speak to many people about the Christian faith, they have little clue what we are talking about. They have not been exposed to it at all and have certainly not seen any of it in action in the real world. So we have to resort to shouting the Good News to them across the void. It is evangelism at a distance — "bargepole evangelism," we might call it.

In contrast, the early Christians were able to evangelize more easily because they worked out their faith in the everyday world. They demonstrated it by their actions and refused to retreat into "holy huddles." We know both from the New Testament and from other writings that the Christians were fully involved in the life of society and in touch with its leaders and decision-makers. What is more important, they took their "private" faith fully into the public arena. They refused to keep it out of public affairs because they believed that Jesus had brought the Kingdom of God to the kingdoms of men and women. They did not keep their spiritual lives in a distinct compartment. Nor should we. We must learn again how to affect both our neighbours, and the public and moral climate of our society, with the Good News of Jesus. It is part of our responsibility and it is vital for the next stage in the continuing process of evangelism.

Evangelism as proclamation

Originally, the word "evangelize" meant "to announce good news." We need to explain clearly to people the content of the Good News we have to share. Evangelism may well be indirect or oblique. The things we do may speak of Christian values and truths in relation to the workaday world. But evangelism as proclamation is much more direct.

Many in our society simply do not know the basic truths of the Good News. They have never been in any real contact with a church or a group of Christians for long enough to find out about them. We often make the mistake of assuming that people have much more knowledge about Jesus than they actually do. To tell the facts of his life, teaching, death, resurrection, and return, and to explain their implications and meaning, is the central task of evangelism.

The word "proclamation" should not be misunderstood as implying that evangelism must be the public announcement to a group, that is, preaching. Proclamation simply means to make known. It does not necessitate a particular style but can refer as much to quiet conversation as public declamation.

Evangelism as persuasion

A third aspect of evangelism is evident in the New Testament. The announcement of the Good News was never made with an indifferent attitude. The New Testament evangelist was determined to persuade his hearers of the truth of what he was saying... to urge them to accept it, with all its implications, as the foundation for their lives. Of course, it was done sensitively. The unfair tactics of deceptive, emotional, or forced persuasion were rejected. But the evangelists were prepared to discuss and debate the matter on their hearers' ground if it would give them an opportunity to tell them about Jesus.

Provoking a response

It is evident, too, that whenever they engaged in evangelism they expected to provoke a response from their listeners, and they expected them to respond both positively and negatively. Some would believe, others would reject, and some would go on thinking. They were not prepared to wait until they got the right formula before they went out to preach. They knew that some would reject their message — that was a sign of God's judgement — and they were prepared for it. They did not believe they could successfully persuade everyone to accept the truth. But there was no thought in their minds that the Good News would be met with indifference. They were too convinced of its relevance and too persuasive in their witnessing not to overcome mere lethargy.

It should be the same for us today. We need to empathize with the way those who are not Christians think and feel, so that we might discuss Christian truth and persuade them of the Good News of Jesus. We too should expect a response and yet be prepared for our message to be rejected.

Methods of evangelism

Three elements are fundamental to evangelism and underlie any and every method which may be adopted. Evangelism involves the *people* of God, filled with the *spirit* of God, taking the *word* of God to those who do not follow Christ. The people and the Holy Spirit work in a close co-operation: both use the word of God (by which we mean God's written word, preaching, and the example of a Christian way of life) as the basic ingredient of their method, as we shall see in the next chapter. We may represent this diagrammatically:

Few restrictions

Within this framework the desire to persuade people about the truth of the Good News led the early Christians to adopt a variety of methods of evangelism. Mass meetings were often the result of a miracle or some opposition rather than deliberate planning. In addition, representations to the authorities, demonstrations, public lectures, house meetings, church worship, and personal conversation were all methods of evangelism used in New Testament times. There seemed to be no rigid restrictions on the methods which were considered legitimate. Most situations seemed capable of being turned into opportunities to start talking about Jesus.

One-to-one evangelism

Michael Green has made a careful study of methods of evangelism in the New Testament church. He has concluded that the most surprising thing is how little, in fact, people used public meetings and how much evangelism happened through ordinary Christians sharing their faith with their friends and neighbours. It was not so much that New Testament church members organized special programmes or events to reach particular groups within their communities. It was the natural outcome of having had their own lives changed by God. The strengths of this approach were numerous.

Evangelism took place whether specialists were there to do it or not. It reached into parts of society where no preacher would have gained access. It concentrated on families rather than particular groups or generations. Above all, the Good News was much more convincing because it was shared by ordinary believers, who could speak about its importance in their own lives.

We shall see that a wide range of methods of evangelism can be adopted which have the Bible as their corner-stone. But, unless sharing the Good News becomes the delight of ordinary Christians, little will be accomplished by some of the methods recommended.

MOTIVES FOR EVANGELISM

The New Testament provides at least four reasons for engaging in evangelism.

A matter of obedience

Almost the last words of the risen Lord to his disciples were:

> *Go, then, to all peoples everywhere and make them my disciples: baptize them in the name of the Father, the Son, and the Holy Spirit, and teach them to obey everything I have commanded you.*
>
> *(Matthew 28.19–20)*

This great commission was no isolated request on the part of Jesus. It combines with his commandments to love our neighbours (Matthew 22.39) and to imitate his own mission (John 20.21), in order to make what he expects of his followers abundantly clear.

People cannot claim to be followers of Jesus unless they do what he tells them to do. On its own this seems a daunting obligation, but the context of Jesus' words in Matthew 28 reminds us that, if we obey, we shall discover his authority is available to us, and his presence within us.

An expression of gratitude

The idea that the early Christians evangelized out of a sense of obligation does not seem to square with the Acts of the Apostles. It is apparent, in Acts and elsewhere, that they envangelized much more out of a sense of gratitude for what God had done for them. Evangelism was an expression of their praise and thankfulness. They shared the Good News because they were inwardly motivated by the Holy Spirit rather than outwardly compelled by a commandment. Evangelism is too often presented as a burden and not recognized as the privilege it is.

An indication of concern

The early Christians felt concerned to rescue their fellow citizens from the present state of their lives, and their future prospects at the last judgement. They wanted to pass on the fact that the quality of life on earth could be improved if people turned to God and that they could experience something infinitely better in the after life if only they would accept God's way. To have failed to share a message which they knew to be vital to the well-being of others would be no less than criminal. The early Christians could not be silent, but had to share the Good News. This is well expressed in D.T.Niles' definition: "Evangelism is one beggar telling another where to find bread."

A recognition of judgement

Paul wrote most passionately about evangelism just after mentioning that every Christian would one day face judgement for the way they had spent their lives (2 Corinthians 5.10). He wrote, "We know what it means to fear the Lord, and so we try to persuade others" (verse 11). It may not be the best of motives, but most of us need the warning of some future inspection as an incentive to do our present work well. Paul was conscious of the most rigorous inspection ever. He was also conscious that it was going to be a judgement about the most important issue ever. What an offence it will have been to be the possessor of such marvellous Good News, which God has given at such a great cost, and which is so desperately needed by others, only to have kept it to ourselves.

CONCLUSION

In short, evangelism is the task of sharing the Good News about Jesus, which the risen Lord himself committed to every one of his followers. It happens at many levels and takes many forms, but the common thread is the spreading of what God has done for a sinful world in Jesus Christ.

2. SHARING GOOD NEWS YESTERDAY

No period in the history of the church has been as effective in evangelism as the New Testament period. The church has never grown as rapidly as it did then. So it is worth looking carefully at that evangelism, to see what lessons can be learned.

WHO DID IT?

Three groups can be identified: the apostles, the evangelists and ordinary members.

The apostles

To begin with, evangelism was done by the apostles. This was simply because they were the eyewitnesses of the life, death, and resurrection of Jesus. There were no other great personal qualifications involved. When Jesus commissioned them, he simply said, "You will be witnesses for me in Jerusalem, in all Judaea and Samaria, and to the ends of the earth" (Acts 1.8). And when they were looking for a replacement for Judas they were concerned that it be a person who had been an eyewitness to everything in Jesus' public ministry. Their message was simply what they had heard and seen concerning Jesus. Look at Acts 2.32; 3.15; 5.32; 10.39, 41; 13.31.

The apostles were not only the original preachers in Jerusalem but pioneer missionaries who planted churches in nearly all the major cities and towns of the ancient world. The outstanding example of this is seen in the apostle Paul. Like the others, he was anxious to show that, even though he was not a member of the original group of apostles, he too was a witness to the resurrection of Jesus (1 Corinthians 15.8).

The evangelists

It was inevitable that with the success of the church and the passing of time the apostles would be unable to retain their position as the almost exclusive witnesses. The task had to be shared. So early on, men like Stephen (Acts 6.8–7.60) and Philip (Acts 8.5–6, 26–40) became evangelists — that is, preachers of the Good News. They were also witnesses in their way, but rather than being first-hand witnesses they were witnesses to what the apostles taught and to the way in which their own lives had verified the Good News about Jesus.

Evangelism was recognized in the early church as a spiritual gift (Ephesians 4.11). The people given this gift had the ability to announce the gospel so clearly that it provoked a response, with some coming to believe in Jesus Christ as a result. Hand in hand with the gift went the irrepressible desire to preach that Good News.

The ordinary members

The task of spreading the Good News was not confined to the apostles and evangelists. "Ordinary" Christians evangelized right from the beginning (Luke 24.35) and there is a good deal of evidence to suggest that it was because of them that the church spread as rapidly as it did. Their witnessing was effective because it was enthusiastic and provoked none of the suspicion usually associated with the "professional." Like the others, they were witnesses. They could not help being so. An eyewitness in a court of law does not need to have undergone a special course before becoming a witness. He or she is a witness simply because of what they saw or heard. So it is with Christians. They are witnesses simply because of what they have seen and heard about God in their lives.

We see something of this in Acts 8.4 where, talking about the aftermath of a campaign of persecution, Luke says, "The believers who were scattered went everywhere, preaching the message." Later on Origen, one of the early church fathers, wrote a book to try to refute Celsus' attacks on Christianity. In it he parodies Celsus' sarcastic complaint about the early Christians.

We see in private houses workers in wool and leather, laundry workers and the most illiterate and bucolic yokels, who would not dare to say anything at all in front of their elders and more intelligent masters. But they get hold of children privately, and any women who are as ignorant as themselves. Then they pour out wonderful statements... (and) win them over.

"3-P" evangelism

In the last chapter I suggested that evangelism takes place on three levels — the levels of presence, proclamation, and persuasion. Each of these is to be found in the New Testament.

Evangelism as presence

The Good News would not have taken hold as it did if it were not for the remarkable quality of life lived by the ordinary Christian. No preacher would have made headway unless the morals, attitudes, and behaviour of ordinary people showed the truth of what they preached. So, the New Testament letters are full of encouragements to engage in "life-style evangelism."

"Presence" evangelism was seen in a more dramatic way too. Miracles were not performed as a way of attracting the attention of the crowd but as a compassionate visual demonstration of the Good News that was proclaimed. According to Acts such demonstrations were often effective on their own as a means of evangelism. Look at this example:

> *Many miracles and wonders were being performed among the people by the apostles...Nobody outside the group dared to join them, even though the people spoke highly of them. But more and more people were added to the group — a crowd of men and women who believed in the Lord.*
>
> *(Acts 5.12-14)*

Evangelism as proclamation

The most prominent method of evangelism in Acts is proclamation. Wherever the chance presented itself, Christian preachers announced the Good News about Jesus. Take Peter's speech on the Day of Pentecost (Acts 2.14–36) or in the Temple (Acts 3.12–26) or in court (Acts 4.8–12) as examples.

After a careful examination of this early preaching the scholar C.H.Dodd claimed to have identified the recurring elements in their proclamation. He said they preached:

- That the messianic age had dawned.
- That it had arrived through the ministry, death, and resurrection of Jesus Christ.
- That Jesus had been exalted, through the resurrection, and had become the messianic head of a new Israel.
- That the Holy Spirit in the church was a sign of Christ's power and glory.
- That the new age would be consummated in the return of Jesus.
- That repentance was needed, forgiveness and the Holy Spirit offered, and salvation promised.

Evangelism as persuasion

But more was involved. Simply announcing the Good News was not enough. It is said of Paul, in Acts 19.8, that he "went into the synagogue and during three months spoke boldly with the people, holding discussions with them and trying to convince them about the Kingdom of God". The first part of this verse speaks about evangelism as proclamation, but the second is about evangelism as persuasion. Other references, for example Acts 17.4 or 18.4, suggest that this was characteristic of Paul's approach. It was certainly clear to Paul's opponents that he was convinced that his message was true and was determined to persuade others to agree with him.

The Good News was announced and every legitimate argument in its favour was produced. The discussions were careful, detailed, and sometimes, as at Ephesus, lengthy. It was all worth it if people were persuaded to follow Jesus.

Their use of the Old Testament

In the New Testament both proclamation and persuasion evangelism make heavy use of the Old Testament scriptures. In proclamation evangelism the Old Testament is a basic ingredient in the announcement. In persuasion evangelism the Old Testament is a basic weapon in the argument. An examination of why and how the New Testament evangelists used Scripture will be helpful to us in our understanding of how we can use it today. It will show that its value is by no means confined to use among the Jewish people of the first century.

The Ministry of Jesus

Jesus' actions during the walk to Emmaus with two of his followers provided the disciples with both a model and a precedent for
using the Old Testament in their evangelism. The disciples were
sad and, having listened to their reasons for feeling as they did,
Jesus said to them:

> *"How foolish you are, how slow you are to believe everything
> the prophets said! Was it not necessary for the Messiah to suffer
> these things and then to enter his glory?" And Jesus explained
> to them what was said about himself in all the Scriptures, begin-
> ning with the books of Moses and the writings of all the
> prophets.*
>
> *(Luke 24.25–27)*

Before long they recognized Jesus and returned to Jerusalem to
share their Good News. Luke seems to make a particular point of
the role the Scriptures played in their experience. It wasn't the
only factor, but he records, "They said to each other, 'Wasn't it
like a fire burning in us when he talked to us on the road and
explained the Scriptures to us?'" (verse 32).

Jesus used the same technique later that evening with the disciples in Jerusalem. We read that Jesus said to them, "'These are the
very things I told you about while I was still with you: everything
written about me in the Law of Moses, the writings of the
prophets, and the Psalms had to come true.' Then he opened their
minds to understand the Scriptures…" (Luke 24.44–45).

New interpretation

Already in his early life Jesus had frequently used the Scripture in
his teachings. He often took an Old Testament text and got people
to look at it in a new way. The texts had often been interpreted by
others many times, so that their real meaning had been completely
obscured. An example of this can be found in part of the Sermon
on the Mount in Matthew 5.21–48. Each paragraph begins with a
quotation from the Old Testament. In several cases an additional
phrase, a human interpretation, had been added, often by a Rabbi,
without so much as a comma in between, which twisted the meaning. Jesus wanted to let his disciples know the original meanings.

Headings

In other cases Jesus used a text almost as a heading for a sermon and then went on to explain it, as in Matthew 15.3. Sometimes he used an Old Testament illustration to justify his teachings, as in Mark 2.25–26. Sometimes it was an Old Testament picture which he developed. His claim to be the Good Shepherd, for example, is a deliberate one, made with the immense implications of Ezekiel 34 in mind. Several times he alludes to himself as the Old Testament servant of the Lord, using the imagery of Isaiah 53. Then again, the Old Testament was introduced to prove a point in an argument with the Pharisees, as happens a lot in John's Gospel. You only have to look at the references at the bottom of the page in a *Good News Bible* to see how often Jesus made use of the Old Testament. So in their use of the Bible in evangelism, the early Christian preachers were simply following the pattern set by their Lord.

EARLY CHRISTIAN PREACHING TO JEWS

The evangelistic sermons of the early Christian preachers recorded in the Acts of the Apostles are peppered with quotations from the Old Testament. Peter's sermon on the Day of Pentecost (Acts 2) is a prime example. In it he quotes from Joel 2.28–32; Psalms 16.8–11, 132.11, 110.1; and 2 Samuel 7.12–13. Out of twenty-two verses twelve are quotations from the Old Testament!

The purpose of this approach is clear. It was to convince Jews that Jesus was the fulfilment of the Old Testament prophecies concerning the Messiah and that the new age in which the Messiah was to rule had arrived.

Septuagint

New Testament writers often quoted from the Septuagint, that is, a Greek translation of the Old Testament made some two hundred years before Christ (see the list at the end of most *Good News Bibles*). Sometimes the writers would quote from memory and they would usually follow correct tradition (especially rabbinic tradition). These writers quoted from those passages which they believed pointed to Christ. They did not provide commentaries on whole books, as they did at Qumran, but rather explained those bits of the Old Testament that were relevant to their evangelism. Nonetheless, although they only used parts of Old Testament books, they often had the context of the whole passage in mind. In a nutshell, they were interested in conveying their message rather than being completely precise as they quoted.

In some cases the early Christians may have used a list of proof-texts as a help in proclaiming Jesus as the Messiah. Such a list would have been useful in a day when manuscripts were not widely available. But the early Christians did more than just quote odd verses. They also used the Old Testament to argue a case. It was quite usual for Jews to take an Old Testament text and re-think it in the light of contemporary events, giving it a clearer meaning for the times than was probably apparent to its original author. The Christians did just this in respect of Jesus. Paul's sermon in Antioch of Pisidia, which is recorded in Acts 13.16–41, is an illustration of this approach. In showing how the whole history of the Jews pointed forward to the coming of Jesus Christ, he quotes from Psalm 2.7, Isaiah 55.3, and Psalm 16.10, and makes all those ancient comments, which initially were taken to refer to something else, point to Jesus.

Referring to the Old Testament was so common that we can fairly conclude it was the principal means by which Jews were made to think about the Good News.

EARLY CHRISTIAN PREACHING TO GENTILES

To state that the first Christian evangelists relied heavily on the Old Testament in their witnessing to Jews is perhaps not surprising. It was the obvious thing to do. The early Christians shared a common religious background and cultural heritage with the Jews and it would have been foolish not to exploit it. But this was not the case with Gentiles. They did not have a Jewish background. So what use did the early Christians make of the Bible in evangelizing them? Was it a viable tool when the background of the Old Testament was absent and a different world of religious thought was encountered?

Acts records two examples of Christian preaching to Gentile audiences, one at Lystra and the other in Athens. At first sight neither seems to have involved the use of the Old Testament and they do not seem to encourage us to use the Bible where it is not already a part of a people's culture. It is true that neither sermon quotes the Old Testament, but to say that it was not used would be a premature judgement.

At Lystra

Look at the account of what happened at Lystra, which is found in Acts 14.8–20. Lystra was a sleepy village eight or ten miles off the nearest trade route, inhabited by superstitious and uneducated people. They believed that Zeus and Hermes had once visited the peasants of the area and it was natural for them, steeped as they were in idolatry, to think they had reappeared when Paul and Barnabas healed the lame man. Paul uses the opportunity to preach and although his message is the same, in essence, as it would have been in any Jewish synagogue, he adapts its presentation to suit the audience in front of him. He has to start right at the beginning, by talking about the one "Living God".

Paul does not quote the Old Testament directly in this short address. But you only have to look carefully at what he says to realize that every sentence of it derives from the Old Testament. The stupidity of idolatry recalls Psalm 115.4–8; 135.15–18; Isaiah 44.9–20, and Jeremiah 10.1–11. The phrases used to refer to God as creator and sustainer recall Genesis 8.22; Exodus 20.11; Psalm 147.8; Ecclesiastes 9.7; Jeremiah 5.24 and so on. In the end it shows that what matters most is Bible-based evangelizing rather than word-for-word quotation of Scripture. Paul's address here is certainly biblical. Every phrase of it is soaked in Scripture.

In Athens

Athens was a very different place to Lystra. Paul's visit to the intellectual centre of his world is spoken of in Acts 17.16–34. The people he faced there were also idolaters. They certainly did not have a background in Jewish monotheism. If anything, they believed in more gods than the people at Lystra. But the idolatry at Athens had a more philosophical bent to it. People were just as superstitious as the common peasants but they covered it up well by clothing it in an intellectual disguise.

Paul showed tremendous cultural sensitivity when he preached to them. He quoted, not from the Old Testament, but from Greek, and he used their two main schools of philosophy, Epicurean and Stoic, to his own ends. The theme of his message was the same as at Lystra, but this time Paul quickly got to the heart of the Good News. He told them that the ultimate proof of what he was saying was found in the resurrection of Jesus.

Once again he is laying the necessary foundation for the preaching of the Good News without quoting from the Old Testament. But again, the strains of Old Testament passages are to be heard in what he says. Look through the passage and you will see reference to Deuteronomy 32.3; Psalm 50.12; 145.18; Isaiah 42.5; 55.6, and Jeremiah 23.33.

In preaching to Gentiles, then, the early evangelists did not abandon Scripture. They used the Old Testament to good effect in their evangelism, even when people were not familiar with it. All they did was leave out the quotation marks.

In church history

We know that this approach to evangelism in pagan areas continued in the subsequent history of the church. Early church leaders often wrote their own evangelistic tracts but many, like Aristides, advised that on finishing the tract the reader should turn to the Bible to read more. The famous early preacher, John Chrysostom, advocated the use of the Bible as containing all that necessary for a man to know if he was to be persuaded to follow Jesus. The great bishop, Augustine, was converted through reading the Bible. The Bible remained the chief tool for evangelism among the Jews and the Gentiles alike.

Why they used the Old Testament

The obvious reason is that the Old Testament was the only part of our Bible which the very early Christians were able to refer to. The New Testament had not yet been written. But it has been suggested that there were three more serious reasons why the New Testament Christians used the Old Testament to support what they were saying. Its tradition, histories, and revered sayings of respected men all helped them.

Secondly, it called forth a cluster of associations and ideas. In pin-pointing something a whole range of other things were brought nearer and into focus. It provided the listener will all sorts of references and allusions to think about later. Thirdly, it was often a much better way of expressing things than the evangelist would have been able to find if left on his own.

Influence and authority

To the reasons given above we may add that the words of Scripture carry an influence and authority all their own. As the second-century Christian leader Justin Martyr put it,

> *I would wish that all, making a resolution similar to my own, do not keep themselves away from the words of the saviour. For they possess a terrible power in themselves and are sufficient to inspire those who turn aside from the path of rectitude with awe; while the sweetest rest is afforded those who make a diligent practice of them.*

3. WHAT IS THE GOOD NEWS?

The Scottish preacher James Stewart once wrote, "The first axiom of effective evangelism is that the evangelist must be sure of his message. Any haziness or hesitation there is fatal." The Bible is like an orchestra playing a magnificent symphony. The instruments do not all sound like each other and yet they contribute to a splendid harmony. Underneath the diversity of music and instrument lie certain basic themes to which they constantly return.

AN OUTLINE

It is our purpose here to outline the basic themes of the Good News, so we may firmly grasp its message. Only after that is done should we be concerned to try and go beyond the basics and present the message in a more personal and varied way.

The outline below is my attempt to summarize the content of the Good News. It's possible you would prefer a different starting point. For instance, you might feel you would want to start with Jesus if you are talking to someone who has no real concept of God. Jesus might be a better person to begin with than God the Father, because people often find it easier to relate to someone who has lived on earth. His life often commands a respect from people who know little of him and provokes a fascination which can be developed further.

Or, you may be uncertain as to whether you should start with God's judgement or with God's love. It might be that you will want to start with God's love, as this is often a familiar concept to people. They tend to see God as a sort of celestial Santa Claus, so it helps to start with something they know and then tell them something that they need to know — that God is holy and righteous. But in whatever order you choose to present it, this is the Good News.

THE GOOD NEWS ORIGINATES WITH GOD

In the ancient world the early evangelists could often assume some understanding of God, particularly if they were talking to Jews. So, often they could immediately start talking about Jesus Christ. Today we cannot make that assumption. We need to ensure that either at the start or sometime later we unpack people's ideas about God and present some basic Christian truths about him.

God made us

We are not the product of the chance forces of nature but the creation of a personal God, who made us to enjoy a close relationship with him. This is the teaching of the early chapters of Genesis. But God's role did not end at the creation. His work is still vital for the continuance of the universe and the maintenance of individual life.

> *God, who made the world and everything in it, is Lord of heaven and earth and does not live in made-made temples. Nor does he need anything we can supply by working for him, since it is he himself who gives life and breath and everything else to everyone.*
>
> *(Acts 17.24,25)*

God judges us

As our creator, God has the right to tell us how we should live. He knew how we could get the best out of life. But humankind wanted to be independent of God and chose to go its own way. Not only has that ruined God's world and spoiled people's lives, but it has offended God himself, who is holy and just. He cannot be indifferent to evil and holds humans accountable for sin. Habakkuk said of God, "Your eyes are too holy to look at evil, and you cannot stand the sight of people doing wrong" (Habakkuk 1.13b). God says, "The life of every person belongs to me...the person who sins is the one who will die" (Ezekiel 18.4).

God loves us

This teaching about God's holy justice should not be taken to mean that he is keen to write off his creation. Amazingly, the Bible speaks of God who, in spite of everything, continues to love and seeks to win them back to himself. "God is love" (1 John 4.8) is the ultimate statement about the nature of God. "The mountains and hills may crumble, but my love for you will never end" (Isaiah 54.10).

God saves us

God's love is not an impotent emotion but a driving force, which causes him to step into the world in order to rescue his people from their plight. He wants to rescue his people and is powerful enough to do so. He did it dramatically for the children of Israel at the time of their exodus from Egypt, but that was only the most spectacular of Old Testament events to illustrate God's continuing "rescue mission." Salvation is the basic message of the whole Bible and is not now limited to a particular nation. Through the death of Jesus it is available to all humankind. "I alone am the LORD, the only one who can save you" (Isaiah 43.11). "I am the LORD, the one who saves you and sets you free...I am Israel's powerful God" (Isaiah 49.26).

THE GOOD NEWS SPEAKS ABOUT HUMAN BEINGS

It has been said that every night television news readers begin by saying "Good evening" and then proceed to tell us why it isn't. Listening to the daily news it is clear there is more bad news than good. In the Christian message bad news does not predominate, but what there is, is necessary. Only as we grasp the bad news are we likely to want the good news. If we do not know the bad news we may feel that nothing is wrong and so have no incentive to search for a solution. It is a bit like going to the doctor and discovering we have a serious illness. It's not a pleasant experience. But at least that way we have a chance of being cured. If we remained ignorant of our true condition, the illness might progress and become terminal. Bad news can lead to good news.

People are sinful

As God's creatures, people have much to offer and life is full of potential. But we have a fatal flaw. Our environment, our heredity, and our own deliberate choices conspire to make us rebel against God and break his commandments. "As the Scriptures say: 'There is no one who is righteous...All have turned away from God; they have all gone wrong; no one does what is right, not even one'" (Romans 3.10,12). "Everyone has sinned and is far away from God's saving presence" (Romans 3.23).

People are guilty

Sin is not only our misfortune, it is our fault and God holds us accountable for it. God's verdict on everyone's life is "guilty" and the sentence is death. Romans 6.23 says, "For sin pays its wage — death; but God's free gift is eternal life in union with Christ Jesus our Lord".

People are incapable

The Bible clearly teaches that there is nothing humankind can do to help itself. Since the standard God requires us to reach is the standard of perfection, none of us, however good or religious we may be, have a chance. Worship, prayer, and doing good, right as they are in themselves, are never enough to reconcile us to God. Paul says, "For it is by God's grace that you have been saved through faith. It is not by the result of your own efforts, but God's gift, so that no one can boast about it" (Ephesians 2.8–9). And "It was not because of any good deeds that we ourselves had done, but because of his own mercy that he saved us" (Titus 3.5).

THE GOOD NEWS CENTRES ON JESUS

What was impossible for us to do for ourselves, God did for us through Jesus Christ. God did not wait for us to improve or to help ourselves before he came to the rescue. This is the central point of the Good News. "But God has shown us how much he loves us — it was while we were still sinners that Christ died for us!" (Romans 5.8).

Who he was

Jesus was both fully human and fully divine. He was the God-man.
John makes fantastic claims about this man who was born in
Bethlehem. He says of him that, "Before the world was created,
the Word already existed; he was with God and he was the same as
God" (John 1.1). Then he goes on to say, "The Word became a
human being". (John 1.14).

How he lived

From any viewpoint and by any standards Jesus' life was remarkable. He was extraordinary however you looked at him: in his
character, in his teaching, and in his actions. Through his own person he made God known and brought us nearer to him. Through
his authoritative teaching he made truth known. Through his
miraculous acts he demonstrated salvation and brought it within
the reach of ordinary people. He could claim himself to be "The
way, the truth, and the life" (John 16.4) and there were many who
had reason to agree. When John wanted to sum up what he thought
of Jesus' life he wrote, "The Word became a human being and, full
of grace and truth, lived among us. We saw his glory, the glory
which he received as the Father's only son. Out of the fullness of
his grace he has blessed us all, giving us one blessing after another" (John 1.14, 16).

Why he died

The significance of Jesus is seen most clearly in his death.
Everyone dies, so it may seem absurd to ask why Jesus died. But
the unusual nature of his death alerts us to probe its meaning more
deeply. According to the Bible, everyone dies as a result of their
sin, but this man was perfect. He died not for his own sins but to
take away the sins of others. Mark puts it like this: "He came to
serve and to give his life to redeem many people" (Mark 10.45b).
Peter puts it in these terms: "Christ himself carried our sins in his
body to the cross" (1 Peter 2.24). And again, "For Christ died for
sins once and for all, a good man on behalf of sinners, in order to
lead you to God" (1 Peter 3.18). Whilst Paul says the same thing in
these words: "By his sacrificial death we are now put right with
God" (Romans 5.9).

Why he rose

Jesus' resurrection was no optional extra. It was an essential part of God's way of securing salvation for us. His death secured our forgiveness, but his resurrection assures us that our worst enemies have been thoroughly routed. If Jesus had remained dead we would never know whether he was stronger than death, or whether death was stronger than him. If he had remained dead we would never have been able to be sure whether good or evil had won at Calvary. But the resurrection leaves us in no doubt that our salvation is real and that he has triumphed over our enemies! Because of Jesus' resurrection Christians should think of themselves as "Living in fellowship with God through Christ Jesus" (Romans 6.11).

What he offers

Jesus is the only way to God. The Christian idea of salvation is unique among the religions of the world. But the Christian claims more than a unique idea. Jesus Christ alone makes salvation effective. "Salvation is to be found through him alone; in all the world there is no one else whom God has given who can save us" (Acts 4.12).

THE GOOD NEWS INVOLVES THE HOLY SPIRIT

Peter finished his sermon on the day of Pentecost by promising that those who received his message would also "receive God's gift, the Holy Spirit" (Acts 2.38). The Spirit is the greatest gift a Christian receives and the bearer of all the other gifts, such as forgiveness, joy, peace, and progressive victory over sin which the Christian experiences. It is important that we do not omit the Holy Spirit and the part he plays when we are telling the Good News.

He makes past facts live

The work of Christ took place at a specific time in history, long ago. But those events are made alive to us today by the work of the

Holy Spirit. Jesus said that he is "the Spirit…who reveals the truth about God" (John 16.13). His work is not just a matter of stating facts or sharing knowledge, but inwardly convincing men and women of the rightness of what Christ did (John 16.8–11). He makes God real to us and assures us of our inclusion in God's family (Romans 8.14–16).

He makes future hope sure

The full extent of our salvation cannot be experienced on earth. We can only know it after death or after Christ has returned to make a new heaven and a new earth. Nonetheless, our hope is not just wishful thinking. The Holy Spirit is the guarantee that we will experience salvation to the full. All this was in Paul's mind when he wrote, "The Spirit is the guarantee that we shall receive what God has promised his people, and this assures us that God will give complete freedom to those who are his. Let us praise his glory!" (Ephesians 1.14).

THE GOOD NEWS INVITES A RESPONSE

The Good News must be acted upon if it is to be of any use. It does not apply automatically. Nor does God force it on people against their wills. Here is an outline of how we should respond to it.

Turn from

When Peter was asked how to become a Christian he began by saying, "Each one of you must turn away from his sins" (Acts 2.38). To become a Christian involves turning away from one's previous lifestyle and rejecting its attitudes and sinful behaviour. No-one can claim to be a Christian whilst wilfully continuing to sin. Turning one's back on sin is an expression of sorrow and apology to God for the way we have lived and the hurt we have caused Christ. The Bible speaks of this as "repentance" (the Greek word means literally to have a "change of mind"). We have a new mind about our lives, our sin, and our need for God.

Turn to

We always turn to face the giver when we receive a gift. But the invitation of the Good News to turn to Christ is not talking about what we do physically but what we do spiritually. Turning to Christ means that we accept that his is the only possible way of salvation. It means, too, that we ask him and trust him to make us right with God. Faith is not just the acceptance of certain truths. There are certain truths which all Christians accept, but that is not where faith begins. Faith is essentially a personal trust in Jesus Christ. When Paul only had a sentence to tell a man how to become a Christian he said, "Believe in the Lord Jesus, and you will be saved" (Acts 16.31).

Turn over

Salvation is not a once and for all experience. The response invited by the Good News is the entry to a new way of life, but that new way of life has many repercussions and implications. Underneath all of them is the need to turn our daily life over to God's control, so that it is lived for him. Once we have done this we will want to begin fostering a relationship with God through worship, prayer, and Bible reading. We will also want to experience fellowship with other Christians by joining a church. "When anyone is joined to Christ, he is a new being; the old is gone, the new has come" (2 Corinthians 5.17).

TO GET YOU STARTED

Something to learn

Try to learn the basic outline of the Good News contained in this chapter and some of the Bible verses which illustrate it.

Something to think about

Look up the story of the conversion of Cornelius in Acts 10.1–48 and see how many points you can identify from the above outline.

Something to do

The outline given of the Good News is only a skeleton. Try to give it flesh and make it more personal by adding to it from your own study of the Bible, and from how you yourself discovered the Good News.

Something to discover

There are many different ways of outlining the Good News. Some of these can be found in the books listed in the Bibliography on p 107. They have proved a great help to many in sharing their faith in Jesus Christ. Why not look at some as well, so that you get a firm grasp of the Good News?

4. MULTI-CHANNEL COMMUNICATION

People communicate in a great variety of ways. Those who want to be heard and understood learn to vary the way in which they present their message. The method they adopt will be determined by several factors, including:

- The message itself.
- The nature of the audience.
- The speaker's relationship with the audience.
- The circumstances at the time.

GOD SPEAKS IN MANY WAYS

So it is with God. The message concerning God's holiness, love, demands, and salvation, are communicated to human beings in a variety of ways. God has never adopted a uniform and unchanging manner of speaking, but, as Hebrews 1.1 puts it, he has spoken "many times in many ways". He even communicates without words. Creation is one of the ways in which God speaks (Psalm 19.1–6). It is a way that everyone can hear, if only they are "tuned in" to receive the message. But the fullest, clearest, and most unambiguous communication of his message came through the life, death, and resurrection of Jesus Christ (Hebrews 1.2; John 1.14).

The Bible

The Bible, too, expresses its message in many ways. Its variety of styles and literature is one of the greatest assets we have in evangelism. Naturally, some parts of the Bible, like the gospels, seem to have an obvious evangelistic purpose and these will be used more often in evangelism than other parts of the Bible. But we should not limit the way in which God speaks, even through the more difficult and obscure books of the Bible. Who would have thought, for instance, that Leviticus would have been an effective evangelistic tool? Who would have chosen Psalm 102.6 as an evangelistic text, or Job as an evangelistic tract? Who would have thought that the genealogy of Jesus in Matthew 1.2–17 would bring someone to faith? Yet, to my certain knowledge, all of these have been used to help individuals get to know Christ.

Of course, it is more appropriate when planning an evangelistic strategy to stick to those passages in the Bible that are most easily used in evangelism. However, the examples above help to show that we should not dismiss parts of the Bible because they are not obviously evangelistic. God can and does speak through all Scripture.

The purpose of this chapter is to review the Bible in order to see how its varying parts may contribute to our evangelism. It will give us a model of good communication, and enable us to see in more detail the message we are to communicate. Then we shall not only be able to use the Bible in a general sense, but direct people to specific parts appropriate to them and their needs.

The categories in which I have chosen to look at the Bible are not exclusive. They should be seen only as rough guides. Obviously the gospels contain history; Revelation is prophecy, and so on. Each category is linked with the next and Scripture needs to be seen as a whole. But the categories in this section will provide useful guidelines as we think about the different kinds of literature contained in the Bible.

God speaks through history

The opening part of the Bible, from Genesis to Esther, records the story of God's people. Many find its long names, its repetitive lists, and its curious details difficult, especially if they lack a knowledge of its historical background. But it need not be so. Within the broad sweep of history it tells the stories of many individuals and shows how God was involved in the ups and downs of their lives and in control of their fluctuating fortunes. The telling of stories has always been and remains a powerful and effective way of communicating a message about values and truths.

These books speak of God's:

- Power
- Commands
- Love

They are useful for:

- Those who want to know whether Christianity has a historical basis or whether it is simply an idea or philosophy. They show God in action in humanity's affairs.
- Those who are intrigued by the Jewish race and wonder what makes them so special. Their history points beyond themselves to the God who chose them.
- Those who want evidence of an active God.
- Those who wish to know about the moral origins and foundations of our society.
- Those who want to see how God deals with individuals and what he has to say about the sufferings and successes of their lives.
- Those who are open to the awesomeness of God.

The New Testament also has its history books. Luke and Acts were expressly written so that the historical foundations of the Christian faith would be recorded and the evidence of eye witnesses be made widely available (Luke 1.1–4). Acts speaks of the "ways that proved beyond doubt" that Jesus rose from the dead (Acts 1.3) and then goes on to detail the amazing birth and growth of the church. For those who want evidence on which to base their faith in Jesus Christ, this is it.

God speaks through poetry

The Bible contains some of the most moving poetry in the world. The Psalms in particular have an amazing ability to capture and express the varied emotions of life. They have enabled many to voice the joys and perplexities of their experiences, which might otherwise have remained locked up inside because of their inability to put their emotions into words.

But they do more them simply express what we feel. In doing so they begin to lead us forward to a new understanding. They so often begin with the problems and puzzles and end with praise. The Psalms refuse to allow the reader to remain wallowing in self-pity or suffering. They help the reader to put his or her experiences in the wider picture of spiritual truth. Because of this it is possible to share appropriate Psalms with people facing particular situations and let the Psalms lead them beyond themselves to God. Here are a few examples. Try using the following Psalms with people who face:

• Suffering and bereavement	23, 30, 102
• Depression and loneliness	41, 42, 74
• Sin and guilt	32, 51, 103
• Stress and insecurity	31, 61, 69, 79, 91, 121, 142
• Injustice and disappointment	10, 17, 37, 52,, 55, 63, 73
• Old age	71, 90
• A search for God	62, 63
• Changing circumstances	107
• Happiness	34, 65, 95, 101

God speaks through philosophy

There are a group of books in the Old Testament which reflect on life and its events and make some very down-to-earth comments about its meanings. They have been known to lead a number who are of a more reflective character to see their need for God.

Job

Job is an account of the anguish of one man who suffers deeply in spite of being a very upright person. He struggles with the gross injustice of his situation and searches for an answer to the profound mystery of suffering. He is unable to solve the riddle himself and finds little comfort in his friends. And yet, through it all, he remains loyal to God.

The book provides no cheap answer to the tragic experiences of life. What it does do is remind us in a powerful way that we are God's creatures and that we are ignorant (Job 38–39). God speaks at the end and, with a dazzling review of his creative powers, convinces Job how wrong it is to question his ways. The plain fact is that we look out on our world from an almost completely self centred position and know only a fraction of true reality. Through his suffering Job encounters God in a new way. Others have done the same, having been motivated by their own suffering to read of Job's experiences.

Proverbs

This collection of sayings has to do with the ordinary affairs of everyday life. It contains saying about:

- Neighbours
- Work
- Gossip
- Time
- Money
- Manners
- Being out of your depth
- Disappointments
- Wives!
- Men!

The *Good News Bible* translates them brilliantly and humorously. At the first sight there is little spiritual content in the sayings, but when one looks again one sees that underlying them all is a conviction that none of these mundane affairs of life are irrelevant to God.

The evangelistic potential of Proverbs lies here. It can help us to see that we make a mess of the way we live because we try to do it without reference to God. To do that is foolish. If we want to live wisely we "must first have reverence for the LORD" (Proverbs 1.7).

Ecclesiastes

This is the most philosophical of writings and discusses the purpose of life itself. The writer tells how he has sought for the meaning of life in all the usual places:

- Pleasure
- Knowledge
- Work
- Power
- Money

He has found them all to be empty. Life seems utterly devoid of purpose. And so it is, unless one follows the clue that he gives right at the end: "Have reverence for God, and obey his commands, because this is all that man was created for" (Ecclesiastes 12.13).

No book speaks more cogently to our world than this one does. (See the author's: *That's Life: Realism and hope for today from Ecclesiastes,* IVP, 1989). Its value lies not only in exposing the bankruptcy of prevailing philosophies of life, but in taking them seriously enough in the first place to discuss them in depth. In this way it leads its reader on to the point of despair, with the result that it creates a hunger for an answer. Only then does it point in the direction of the solution.

God speaks through argument

The Prophets are the most explicit spokesmen on behalf of God in the Old Testament. From Isaiah to Malachi they argue his case with the Jews (Isaiah 1.18). In them, his demands, disappoint-ments, and love do not lie unobtrusively in history; nor are they caught within the flights of poetry, or concealed in the riddle of philosophy. They are unmistakably spelled out for all to hear. These books speak of God's:

- Control of history and his power over nations (Isaiah 40, 45).
- Concern for social justice and personal holiness (Isaiah 58, Amos 5.10–15, Micah 6.6–16).
- Judgement on evil (Jeremiah 46–51, Amos 1–2, Obadiah).
- Explanation for the failure of his agreement with Israel and his punishing them in the exile (Isaiah 50.1,2, Jeremiah 5).
- Persistent love (Hosea 11).
- Salvation, which lies in the coming of the Messiah (Isaiah 53, Jeremiah 31, Ezekiel 16, Zechariah 9.9–17).
- Invitation for the Israelites to return (Isaiah 65, Jeremiah 3, Joel 2.12, 13).

The evangelistic potential of the Prophets lies particularly in the great passages predicting future salvation. In spite of everything, God still loves his people and will take the initiative again in ensuring their deliverance. This means that one special use of the Prophets lies in taking the passages which forecast the coming of the Messiah and using them to convince the Jews that Jesus was that Messiah. That was what many of the New Testament evangelists did. But their use should not be confined to the Jews. They have enormous value as a basis for arguing the faith with sceptical

Gentiles as well. Justice, peace and the integrity of creation are all major contemporary concerns for many. Whilst others need to learn of a God of power, justice, and love, as a background to understanding the Good News of Jesus.

God speaks through gospels

One of the aims of the writers of the four gospels was to spread the Good News. Apart from this, each writer had a number of more specific objectives in mind and probably a distant audience as well. This, together with the individual abilities of the writers, means that each of the gospels has a character of its own. So it is more appropriate to use one gospel in some circumstances than others, although it would be foolish to suggest that there are any iron laws about this.

Matthew

Matthew's Gospel seems primarily to have been written in a Jewish setting. He is specially concerned to portray Jesus as the fulfilment of the Old Testament prophecies concerning the Messiah. He emphasizes Jesus as a teacher, or rabbi, and also stresses his fulfilment of the Jewish Law. He is generally concerned with relating the Good News of Jesus to matters which would have been of particular interest to those who knew the Old Testament well.

It is long gospel but it is very deliberately structured, with passages of teaching alternating with descriptions of events, making it very easy to follow.

Mark

This is the shortest of the gospels. Jesus' life is presented at breath-taking speed and is allowed to speak for itself. One of his favourite words is "immediately". Virtually nothing is said about Jesus before his public life began. In his public ministry, Jesus is shown to be a man of commanding authority, both in his preaching and his actions, who can defeat evil in the world in all its forms. It is also noticeable that Mark spends a disproportionate amount of

time on the death of Christ. But that is the whole point, for salvation comes through the death of Jesus. The gospel was almost certainly written for Gentiles and is free from elements which
demand an understanding of Jewish culture.

It may be the most useful of the gospels in our culture because
of its brevity and style. It is easy to read and does not demand as
much of its readers as the other gospels by the way of background
knowledge.

Luke

It is important to be aware of a number of features about Luke's
Gospel. It has already been mentioned that Luke's concern was to
write an accurate historical record of Jesus' life. But it should also
be noted that Luke records his history with superb artistry. He is a
great story-teller. He recounts more of the parables of Jesus than
the other gospels, including well known ones like that of the Lost
Son. He also writes more about the people Jesus met. He appears
to make special reference to Jesus' concern for non Jews, women,
children, and the socially deprived.

John

John says that his purpose in writing was "that you may believe
that Jesus is the Messiah, the Son of God, and that through your
faith in him you have life" (John 20.31). Many, therefore, have
assumed that John's primary intention is evangelistic and have
used his gospel as their principal evangelistic literature.

There are, however, some difficulties with this view. John's
Gospel is different from the other three in many ways, presenting a
deeper and more reflective view of the life of Christ. It contains
much teaching included in the other gospels, which is valuable for
Jesus' followers but which seems to have little evangelistic bearing. The portrait of Jesus is painted on the widest possible canvas
and locates him in relation to eternity. Its perspective is mystical.

It could be that John was writing to Christians who were "up
against it", to help them go on believing "that Jesus is the
Messiah" (John 20.31). Obviously this is not to say that it should
not be used in evangelism. It has been used too frequently and
with great effect in the past to say that. Moreover, it contains some

very clear statements about the meaning of Christ's coming into the world, such as John 3.16. But rather than using this gospel first in any widespread distribution programme, it is probably better to reserve it, to give to those who are more thoughtful about Jesus.

Choose the gospel carefully

The four gospels are rather like four newspapers reporting the same event. They write about one thing from four different viewpoints and present it in four different styles. Just as people vary in their choice of newspaper, so people will vary in their appreciation of the gospels. To give *The Times* to a person who normally reads *The Sun* will almost certainly mean that the newspaper will be unread. The same is probably true, but not quite so certain, the other way round! So select your gospel with care, matching it to the needs and character of the intended reader.

God speaks through teaching

The remainder of the New Testament consists of letters written to the churches to explain the faith and encourage obedience to Christ. Because there were so many misunderstandings in the first churches about the nature of Christian belief these letters have a role to play in evangelism. The writers have to go over the elementary ground of the faith again and again. In doing so, they give us accounts of the gospel. Take Romans 5.6–11, 1 Corinthians 15.1–8, Ephesians 2.1–10, Colossians 1.15–23, 1 Thessalonians 1.9–10, and 1 Peter 1.3–5, 18–21 and 2.21–25 as just a few examples.

Using pictures

Such passages rarely concern themselves with the details of life or death of Jesus, but they explain the implications of his work by means of abstract concepts. To do this the writers often borrow a picture from the world, with which their readers would be familiar, as a way of explaining what Christ means. So Paul takes a picture from the law courts and says that salvation is just as if God, an incorruptible judge, passes a verdict of "Guilty" on the criminal, but then takes the punishment himself, setting the guilty party entirely free. He takes a picture from the family and talks of becoming a Christian as being adopted or being reconciled. He borrows a picture from the slave market and talks about God paying the price to set us free. Then he looks at humankind's ultimate enemy, death, and describes the heart of the Christian message as having a new life in Christ or experiencing resurrection. Using and explaining these metaphors of salvation means that the New Testament letters need not be restricted in use to those who can think abstractly.

God speaks through Revelation

The book of Revelation was essentially written as an encouragement for Christians who were about to face severe persecution rather than as a detailed forecast of future political events. So Christians should not use it like a crystal ball, as a means of predicting the course of current affairs. Care should be taken not to induce false anxiety in people by the unwise use of the mysterious and frightening creatures and events of which the prophecy speaks. But the book is extremely useful in evangelism for showing:

- That evil is not to be underestimated
- The evil powers which are really at work behind the events of our world
- The way in which God is at work behind the scenes
- The way in which God will triumph over evil
- The promise God holds out for the future
- That Christians base their confidence on the resurrection of Jesus Christ

CONCLUSION

Every part of the Bible, then, has some potential use in evangelism, even if we use (rightly) some parts of it more regularly than others. Try to improve your imagination of the way in which the Bible might be used and try to match particular parts of the Bible to the individual needs of people you know. There is something for everyone in it.

5. CAN WE STILL USE THE BIBLE?

Granted the Bible may have been an excellent tool for evangelism in years gone by, and there may theoretically be several advantages in using its varied presentation of the Christian message, but the question remains, is it practical to use the Bible today? Many fear it is no longer a valid tool and, without stopping to consider the matter further, dismiss it as useless.

THE PROBLEMS OF USING THE BIBLE TODAY

The difficulties of using the Bible today fall into four groups.

Ignorance

You only have to listen to the average radio quiz programme to discover how ignorant people are of the Bible. Panellists seem to know the most obscure facts, but when asked the source of a quotation from the Bible they are often unable to answer. If they answer at all, they are likely to attribute it to Shakespeare. Such people give us a good idea of the ignorance of the Bible within this country today.

About the stories
Bible Society's recent survey, *Attitudes to Bible, God and Church,* warned that preachers could not rely on even a passing knowledge of the Bible in six out of ten of the population. It commented, "We can no longer refer to 'The Prodigal Son' and assume that people will know the story." One evening, a friend of mine was preaching on that mysterious figure Melchizedek from Hebrews 7, when a lady from his estate, who was not a regular churchgoer, came to the service. He regretted that he was not preaching on something more straightforward and tried to make his message clear. He apologized to her afterwards, and offered to explain things further if she wanted him to do so. He was greeted with the reply, "Oh, Melchizedek I understand. You've made that clear. But who's this

Abraham you're on about?" Such stories abound. If we ever were, we are no longer the land of "the Book".

About the background and culture

The problem of ignorance is not confined to the contents of the Bible, but also to its background and culture. Some of this can, and has been, legitimately solved in modern translations of the Bible like the Good News Bible. Weights and measures, for example, can easily be expressed in contemporary terms, thus removing an obstacle to understanding. Where it is not possible to handle the "culture gap" in this way, it is often easy enough to supply background information on such things as life-style, customs, beliefs, history, and geography, which will enable people to understand things more easily.

Literacy

Ignorance of the Bible may well have some connection with the second problem, which is that of literacy. It is said that three million adults (almost 10% of the adult population of England) are virtually illiterate. The current average qualification achieved by school leavers is no more than a low grade in the GCSE examination which possibly suggests that many people leave school with few reading skills and little enthusiasm for reading. These hard facts point to a general feature of our culture. We are no longer book-lovers. Many homes possess few or no books, and when there are some, they are seldom read. The TV, video, hi-fi, and radio have replaced books, not only as the chief means of entertainment, but also as the most attractive tools of education. Even those whose professional job demands a high level of reading at work read little at home. So using the Bible in this context as a means of evangelism may appear to be adopting a strategy deliberately aimed at achieving poor results.

Credibility

The most serious difficulty involved in using the Bible in evangelism is the credibility of the Bible itself. In recent years there has been a widespread questioning of social institutions and authorities which had previously been taken for granted. This has led to a questioning of the moral principles on which the institutions were built. The Bible's credibility has undoubtedly suffered as a result.

People have turned to other authorities, which they believe are capable of offering either a more secure or a more adventurous basis for life. Let's look at some of the problems.

- Science seems to have called into question the Bible's interpretation of the physical basis of life, and the possibility of a supernatural dimension.
- Social sciences have raised doubts about the Bible's moral interpretation of life.
- History has raised questions about the truth of the facts on which the Christian faith is built.
- For others, who know little or nothing of what the Bible says, living life to the full means immediate gratification of desires and a freedom from fuddy-duddy moral restrictions — the type of restrictions they think the Bible contains. And there is a general assumption that the Bible is a boring book and is best left unread.

Answers are possible

These are serious obstacles, and they have been made worse because the church often seems to be unable to answer the charges against the Bible or to be fuelling the accusations. It is imperative that those who wish to use the Bible in evangelism think through their answers. Most of these objections provide the basis for constructive discussion with those to whom we are trying to witness.

Answering such objections can be a long task and it is not the purpose of this book to explain the kinds of answers that are possible. We should spend time reading about these matters and you will find a list of books to help you in the Bibliography (p.107). These will help you think through some answers and use them when speaking to others. Remember that many scientists, social scientists, and historians find no contradiction between their findings and their Christian beliefs. The knowledge and insight to be gained from these disciplines should not be dismissed, for they can provide us with useful pointers to the way the world is and why people react as they do. However, it is important that we use these insights to help our faith grow and not to undermine it or the value of the Bible.

Misconception

Another big problem we face in using the Bible is that many people think they know what it says when they are clearly ignorant of or mistaken about its contents. Their knowledge has been formed on the basis of vague impressions and half-hearted listenings to what someone else has said about it.

There is an urgent need to challenge such attitudes perhaps by gently demonstrating that someone has got part of the Bible's message wrong. The problem is best overcome by appealing to motives which will provoke the person to find out for themselves what the Bible says.

THE POSSIBILITIES OF USING THE BIBLE TODAY

In spite of the problems we have considered, it is still possible to use the Bible today. The problems are only one side of the coin. There is another side to it. Consider, for instance, the following issues.

The Bible and our culture

The Bible is deeply embedded in our culture and is an integral part of our national heritage. Both our language and our literature are full of the imagery of the Bible, even if people do not realize that the Bible is its source. We still speak of "lambs to the slaughter", of "Job's comforters", or "going the second mile", of "doubting Thomases" and of "prodigal sons". Our national life and customs still make frequent use of the Bible. We use it to swear an oath in a court of law and in celebrations of great royal or national events, and it is still, in many ways, an implicit part of our way of life. There remains a great respect for it as a book in which God's view can be known. As the report by Bible Society commented,

> *It is as if the Bible has an intrinsic value recognized by English people and is seen as God's way of communicating with man (or one of his ways). People may not know what the Bible says but still believe that God has somehow spoken through it!*

The Bible and common religion

Although only 10% of the population can be found in church on any given Sunday and only a small minority are committed to church institutions, there is a great deal of residual religious belief in our society, including among the working classes. This can be seen in the much larger proportion of the population who turn to the church during life's transitions and crises, for such things as christenings, weddings, and funerals. A high proportion of people want to feel that they belong to a church, even though they never go. A great number of people pray who would never be visibly identified with the church. Few are prepared to say they do not believe in God and many would claim to have some form of faith. More significant, for our purposes, is the fact that 84% of households possess a Bible and 60% of individuals say they own one. Many Bibles are given as presents every year by people who would not claim to be very religious. The problem seems to be more one of getting people to read the Bible than one of distribution. Even so, we can be encouraged by Bible Society's survey, which estimated that half a million people read the Bible regularly, though they never or hardly ever attend a church. Here is a basis on which to build our evangelism.

The Bible and reading

Although the assertion that we are no longer a book orientated culture contains some truth, it needs to be put into perspective. In 1983, 51,000 new books were published in the United Kingdom. During the same year public libraries made 649 million issues. Each year throughout the 1980s between 102 and 125 fast selling paperbacks sold over 100,000 copies each. A novelist like Jeffery Archer can sell over 1 million copies of his latest book in the first year of publication. When an allowance is made for the number of books bought but not read, or borrowed and returned unopened, someone must still be doing a lot of reading! According to a government survey 83% of homes possessed at least one paperback and only 3% of households had no book at all.

Books may be read rarely in inner city areas of our nation, but even there, once we turn from books to other forms of printed communication we can see just how much people still read. The reading of practical handbooks is widespread. 4,800,000 copies of the 1982–83 AA Handbook were distributed. And what about the Highway Code and the DSS pamphlets, which are distributed on a vast scale? Think, too, of the mass of information being absorbed through newspapers, magazines, signs, posters, and TV. People certainly still read — their welfare, and sometimes even their lives, depend on it. But what they read is often accompanied by a lot of pictures and is certainly easily digestible. Its popular style, visual image and lack of word density is something we still have to learn from.

Presentation

The problem seems to be not whether such people will read but what they will read. Presentation is all important. This emerges from Bible Society's survey, in which the question was asked, "What, if anything, do you think might give you a more favourable view of the Bible?" No very clear picture emerged but a change in language and format was high on the list of suggestions. To use the Bible in evangelism then, demands that we learn how to present it. To distribute densly-worded, thick volumes, with no guides as to how to read them and no pictures, is counter-productive. If we distribute attractive selections, which are well set out and have strong visual impact, and which are not too demanding in the number of words used, we stand a chance of overcoming any obstacle a limited-book culture erects. Quality of presentation is also an important matter because of the amount of junk mail with which it will have to compete for attention.

The Bible and curiosity

One of the other interesting findings in Bible Society's survey concerned why people started to read the Bible. Churchgoers started to read because of their faith in Jesus Christ. Non churchgoers were more likely to start reading out of interest or curiosity. The lives and sayings of great people are of enormous interest and few people have been more influential in history than Jesus. Far from being a barrier, people's ignorance of him could be an asset. They can be invited to find out for themselves what his life and teaching was like, without their minds being cluttered with unhelpful prejudices. It is easier to grow vegetables in clean soil than in a patch of ground covered with weeds. Those who think they already know about Jesus should be challenged to check their facts before agreeing or disagreeing with him.

The Bible and the Holy Spirit

Until now we have been writing about the Bible as if it were just like any other book, but the Bible puts itself in a different category from the rest. Faith is needed if its message is to have effect. The writer to the Hebrews pointed out that the problem with the children of Israel in their wilderness journey was that, although they heard a message from God, "it did them no good, because when they heard it, they did not accept it with faith" (Hebrews 4.2). Yet the same chapter says, "The Word of God is alive and active, sharper than any double-edged sword. It cuts all the way through, to where soul and spirit meet, to where joints and marrow come together. It judges the desires and thoughts of man's heart" (Hebrews 4.12).

No ordinary book

The Bible is no ordinary book, but a book through which God speaks by his Holy Spirit. Peter's first letter demonstrates the close connection between the Spirit and the word of God. The Holy Spirit inspired the first Christians to search the Scriptures and discover in them how God had prepared the way of Christ's coming. He also inspired the spread of the Good News once Jesus had come. (1 Peter 1.11–12; see also 2 Peter 1.21.) Once the Good News has taken root in an individual's life the Holy Spirit continues his work, "For through the living and eternal word of God you have been born again as the children of a parent who is immortal" (1 Peter 1.23). So the Holy Spirit not only inspired the writing of Scripture but inspires its use and effectiveness today. As Jesus himself said.

> And when he [the Holy Spirit] comes, he will prove to the people of the world that they are wrong about sin and about what is right and about God's judgement... When, however, the Spirit comes, who reveals the truth about God, he will lead you into all the truth.
>
> (John 16.8 and 13)

Get people to read it
Using the Bible then, is not like using any other literature, which we hope will persuade people of its truth by the sheer power of

human logic or human inspiration. It is to open up a channel of communication in which God himself is intimately involved. That is why the best answer to those who say they do not believe in the Bible and therefore do not want to read it, is "You don't have to believe it. Just find out first what it says and then decide whether to believe it or not. Dismiss it, but only once you have read it." This exposes them to the work of God. The spirit can then captivate their attention, show them their need, and make known God's love.

The advantages of using the Bible

Research has shown that there is a good deal to be said for using the Bible in evangelism. It is worth considering the following findings:

- Once people have read the Bible they are usually favourably disposed to it.
- People are marginally more favourably disposed to the Bible than they are to the church. They are certainly not hardened against the God of the Bible, although they feel that the church has often failed to communicate its message in any meaningful way.
- Once people read it, the Bible can have a lasting impact on their lives, even if that impact operates at a subconscious level.
- Most people start to read because they were personally invited to do so. Although some are self-motivated and begin to read solely out of curiosity, most are prompted by others.
- The crucial task is to persuade people to read the Bible. Many possess one and have a high level opinion of it, but have never actually read it. Two things might persuade them to do so. First, they might be persuaded because they are impressed by the life of the person who invited them to do so. Second, they might be persuaded by the attractiveness of the publication itself. If they can be persuaded to read they might well encounter God for themselves.

Yes, the Bible can still be used!

Thorough research has recently been undertaken to discover how people find faith (*Finding Faith Today,* by John Finney, Bible

Society 1992). It is very evident from that research that most people find faith through personal relationships – the witness of family, friends or even ministers. But the role of the Bible is not insignificant. 5% reported that reading the Bible was the main factor in leading them to Christ and 27% named it as an important factor on their journey to faith.

By unpacking these bold statistics, other interesting facts emerge. The Bible proved to be more significant for those whose conversions were sudden than for those whose conversions were more gradual. Its role varied according to the denomination the convert was in touch with; and proved to be of greater significance if people were in touch with a denomination that emphasized the place of the Bible in Christian faith.

If the statistics look low, they should be compared with others. The combined figure for those who mentioned the role of the Bible in their conversion as either the most important factor or a major supporting factor made it more significant than the role of parents, evangelistic events, Christian literature, drama, music, TV, audio or supernatural experiences.

Yes! We can still use the Bible in evangelism with good effect.

6. UNDERSTANDING THE BIBLE

If we are to use the Bible confidently in our evangelism we must know and understand it well. It is foolish to imagine that we are adequately equipped for the task simply because we have learned a few texts. A superficial approach like that may well prove quite a hindrance. Anyone can prove anything by stringing together a list of texts. We need to have a mature grasp of the Bible.

BACKGROUND TO UNDERSTANDING

Let me begin with three basic convictions:

1. The best way to become confident about the Bible is to expose ourselves to it. Many people have all sorts of problems, reservations, and prejudices concerning the Bible, which can be overcome once they begin to read it for themselves. Confidence comes from using the Bible, just as confidence in our ability to drive comes as we actually get into the car and drive.

2. The best way to increase our knowledge of the Bible is to read it regularly. Naturally, we shall need some help, but there are plenty of aids to assist us. The point, however, is that we learn best what we engage in most. No one learns to play a musical instrument by an occasional flirtation with it. Regular daily practice is essential to master an instrument. In learning a language the crucial factor is to be constantly adding to your knowledge a little at a time, and using it as regularly as possible. So it is with the Bible. The best way to become familiar with it is to adopt a habit of daily Bible reading, using one or other of the available guides (see addresses at the end).

3. The best way to increase our understanding of the Bible is to study it carefully. The Bible is not altogether an easy book and it does throw up a number of difficulties. Some passages are hard to understand; some seem to contradict others; some only make sense if their background is known, and so on. To grapple with these problems, and to be able to answer adequately some of the questions and challenges we shall receive in the course of our evangelism, it will almost certainly be necessary to go

beyond just reading a daily section of the Bible for one's own benefit. More intensive study is called for. Once again, we are fortunate in having plenty of resources available to help us with that study (see the Bibliography on p.107).

Basic tools

Three basic tools are needed:
- A Bible commentary, which will comment on the meaning and difficulties of passages. There are hundreds in print, varying from one volume commentaries, which cover the whole Bible, to detailed volumes on individual books of the Bible. Some do not assume much knowledge but others can be very technical.
- A Bible dictionary, in which you will be able to look up a topic, person, place, or theme, and immediately find a potted survey of what the Bible says about that topic.
- A Bible concordance, which will list the uses of particular words in the Bible. You could look up "joy", or "salvation", or "Timothy" for example and immediately have access to all the texts in which those words occur. There is now a Concordance to the *Good News Bible,* which will be very helpful if you are using the *Good News Bible* in your evangelism.

GUIDELINES FOR UNDERSTANDING

Although understanding the Bible may not be an easy task it is certainly not an impossible one. Remember, the Bible was not written by scholars for scholars, but mostly by ordinary people, busily engaged in the mission of the church, for ordinary believers. It is a book which has an innate power to communicate with everyone. But if we come to it bearing certain guidelines in mind, we will find that it will yield even more of its meanings to us. We shall discover much more if we keep on asking a number of questions about what we read. What is more, we'll be able to be much more confident we have understood it correctly.

What does it say?

This question sounds idiotically straightforward, but its simplicity may be deceptive. A modern translation of the Bible such as the *Good News Bible* may immediately make the meaning of the words plain, but some of the older translations will not, and some verses will still be difficult. Make sure you understand the meaning of the words used. Are there any words, phrases, or terms you do not understand? If there are, check what is written in your Bible by using a more up-to-date version. Or use a Bible dictionary to help you. If you use another Bible make sure that it is a translation and not a paraphrase, which does not stick quite so close to the original manuscripts.

What does it mean?

The meaning of any language depends on the context in which it is spoken or written. Knowing what the words mean in the abstract is only the beginning of the process of understanding. We must go beyond that and ask what they mean in a particular instance, and to discover that we must look at them in their original setting. This will lead us to ask a number of other important questions about a particular Bible passage:

1. *What do we know about its historical background?*
   Our understanding of so much, perhaps particularly of the Old Testament, depends on our working out who was related to whom, which king ruled where, who won what battles, how long people lived, and so on. But history is not just a collection of dates, kings, and battles. History is about how people used to live, and the more we can understand the social customs of the people of Bible days, the more understanding we shall have of the Bible itself. Without a knowledge of the practice of child sacrifice God's request to Abraham to offer up Isaac seems absurdly sadistic. To place the request in the context of a time when child sacrifice was commonly practised makes it somewhat less absurd. The background to marriage and family customs, practices at the royal court, and an understanding of religious traditions, or of the heresies against which Paul was writing, all help us to better understand the Bible.

2. *What do we know about its world view?*
   How did the original writers of the Bible see their world? Let us take one simple example of what we have in mind. We see our earth as suspended in space and revolving around the sun. But

they saw it as a three-tier construction, with the heavens above, the earth in the middle, and a third layer under the earth. That picture is often alluded to in the Bible. The heavens were thought to be held up on pillars and to form a huge dome overarching the whole earth, which had holes in it and through which the rain occasionally came. The earth was the centre of the universe. The basement under the earth was the place where evil powers lived. To understand that this was how the universe was seen helps us to interpret the meaning of a number of passages in the Bible.

3. *What do we know about its literary style?*
Language is a glorious mosaic, not a dull uniformity. We speak to each other using a colourful diversity of approaches. Sometimes we speak literally, scientifically, and unemotionally. But it would be boring if we always spoke like that. We add colour by speaking metaphorically. We add depth by speaking poetically and we add warmth by speaking emotionally. None of these ways of speaking need cast doubt on the truth of what we say — truth is much too complex to line-up a statement against some test of literacies and measure it for precision.

The Bible makes full use of the metaphoric language (see John 14.6). Whole books are devoted to the language of poetry, of oratory, of parable, and of apocalyptic writing. To understand what we are reading we need to ask what literary style the author is adopting. This is a difficult area and one which has given rise to many arguments. But it is vital that we should grapple with it. To interpret something literally which was written pictorially may cause us to ask all sorts of unnecessary questions about the passage. This is often the case when it comes to our understanding of prophecy. And, of course, to interpret something metaphorically when it was meant literally can cause us to miss the truth we are meant to see.

4. *What do we know about its original purpose?*
An author's intention greatly affects the way in which he writes. It helps to determine what he selects for inclusion and what he omits. It helps to determine the approach he chooses and his style of writing. An understanding of the author's purpose is a tremendous asset when reading the Bible and scholars have contributed much to our understanding in this area.

Let us look at two examples. It is often suggested now that the gospels were written to deal with particular problems in the church as well as being evangelistic documents. Mark, for example, may have been written for the benefit of Christians in Rome who were suffering for their faith. That would partly explain why he emphasizes those parts of Jesus' teaching which concentrate on suffering in the present as a true mark of Christian discipleship. This may also explain why he stresses the example of the suffering of Jesus so much, while he says almost nothing about the parables of Jesus and virtually nothing, for example, about his birth.

To many, the book of Revelation is the most mysterious book in the New Testament. People have managed to read the most amazing contemporary events into it and to come up with the most fanciful interpretations. But often they do so because they have forgotten the key issue with which any interpretation of revelation must start (although not end): that is, why was it written? It was written to encourage Christians who were about to enter a period of fierce persecution, and it was written in an atmosphere where it was impossible to speak openly about such things without being charged with sedition. John, therefore, adopts an almost cartoon-like approach in his writing, so that his reader would be able to recognize what he was talking about without giving explicit interpretations which would provide material for a court case. If we bear in mind that John wishes to encourage suffering Christians, and remember their situation, Revelation loses at least some of its mystery and at the same time increases in both clarity and splendour.

5. *What do we know about its immediate context?*
An important rule in interpreting the Bible is to read individual verses in their context. The Bible did not originally contain chapter and verse divisions and they can sometimes be as much of a hindrance as a help. They tend to isolate statements which belong in the middle of a whole flow of argument, and to separate passages where separation was not intended and may be unhelpful. Always look around the verse you are studying to see its connections. What comes before and what follows? Why is it put just there? What does it say in relation to the whole drift of the passage? These questions will often lead us to a different understanding of the meaning of a verse than the one with which we began.

6. What do we know about its wider context?

The best commentary on Scripture is Scripture itself and we should expect any one part to be understood against the background of the rest. Scripture is a unity, not a random selection of contradictions. This principle will prove its worth in a number of ways. It will prevent us from believing wild doctrines which appear to hold water and discipline us to relate our doctrine to the whole framework of Scripture. It will help us with passages which we do not immediately understand, because it will lead us to start with what we know and use that as a means of interpreting what we don't know. It will help us to understand the relationship between the Old and New Testaments, neither of which are complete on their own. The Old Testament is interpreted and fulfilled by the New Testament, whilst the New Testament is both anticipated by and illustrated by the Old Testament.

How does it apply?

This is the question with which many people start. But, as we have seen, it should be the question which we work towards. If we begin here we are much more likely to come up with some purely private interpretation, which enables us to read anything we like into the Bible.

But it is equally wrong not to ask this question at all. To stop short not only means that the Bible remains unrelated to our lives and unapplied to our society, but that the Bible is prevented from achieving the purpose for which it was written. 2 Timothy 3.16 says, "All Scripture is inspired by God and is useful for teaching the truth, rebuking error, correcting faults, and giving instructions for right living." It has a thoroughly practical concern and this needs to be applied. Once the previous steps have been undertaken we can decide on its relevance by asking a series of simple questions. Here are sixteen examples which could be asked. They are not exhaustive and you might like to add some of your own, but it will help us to ask if there is:

- A truth for me to believe?
- A lesson for me to learn?
- A principle for me to live by?
- A command for me to obey?

- An experience with which I can identify?
- A warning for me to note?
- An example for me to follow?
- A prayer for me to echo?
- A promise for me to accept?
- A sin for me to confess?
- An encouragement for me to take?
- A reason for me to praise?
- A cause for me to fight?
- A goal for me to aim for?
- An action for me to do?
- A policy for society to adopt?

CONCLUSION

The three levels of questions we must always bring to our reading of Scriptures are:

- What does the text say?
- What does the text mean?
- How does the text apply?

If we ask these questions and are prepared to work for answers we shall not only find it of great benefit in our personal and social lives, but in our evangelistic task as well.

7. USING THE BIBLE WITH INDIVIDUALS

The sight of a man walking down a busy street or across a crowd-ed promenade carrying sandwich-boards on which he has some well-chosen texts from the Bible, usually about the end of the world, is not so common now. But it can still be seen. How do you react when you see such a sight? Probably with a good deal of admiration for the man's courage but with a good deal of embar-rassment too. The embarrassment arises because a sandwich-board is such a poor means of communication with the feel of a past age or eccentricity about it. Evangelism is about communicating the Good News of Jesus, so it would be helpful to look at the subject of communication.

A GUIDE TO COMMUNICATION

What is communication?

Communication is not simply about being heard — it is about being understood, and there can be a world of difference between the two. When you begin to think about it, communication is a very complex business. Take a simple example: if I answer my telephone and I am greeted by the words "Hi. It's Steve", I may not be made any wiser. I know several Steves! He only really com-municates with me when I am able to understand which Steve he is. I am sure you have found yourself in the embarrassing position of being part-way through a conversation before you realized you were not talking to the person you thought you were. Communication had failed!

But in his greeting Steve has probably given me a clue as to his identity, for not all the Steves I know would begin with the word "Hi". In any case, his voice will probably give him away, which goes to show that more that just the use of words is involved in communication. The choice of words, the tone of voice, the inflec-tions used, are all important. In most situations too, though not on the telephone, communication is helped by facial expressions and other non-verbal signals.

The process of communication

The old idea that communication involves a speaker pouring out his or her words into passive listeners, rather like pouring water into a bucket, is a very misleading one. Communication is rather a three-stage process at least. It involves a sender, who initiates the message, a transmission, which conveys the message, and a receiver, who interprets the message. If effective communication is to take place all three stages of the process must be working properly.

Language as code

The sender put his or her message into code. Most often we do not realize that this is what we are doing, because we just use plain words, the meaning of which is theoretically open to all to understand. We are using the term "code" in a technical sense here, which even includes ordinary language. But sometimes it is a literal code, like the morse code, or a private language which families invent, or an in-joke which excludes the outsider. In the process of transmission, it is possible that the code will suffer from some sort of interference, so the receiver may not receive what was intended. In any case, once he or she does receive it, they have to decode it; that is, interpret what the message means. Their ability to do so and to understand exactly what the sender meant will depend on them knowing the same code as the sender.

This is the basis of all communication. As an illustration, think of a radio programme. The producers of the programme must choose a language and style of presentation appropriate to the programme's listeners. It is no good speaking in French if their listeners know only English. The programme is then encoded, both in terms of its presentation and in terms of its translations through the air. But think how that transmission might suffer: the transmission could be jammed, another station could stray onto the frequency, or static might cloud its reception. Then the receivers have to be tuned in correctly — not just the radio receivers but the human ones too. The human decoders need the right equipment as much as the electronic ones. They need to listen and be able to understand.

ITS RELEVANCE TO EVANGELISM

The encoder is the evangelist

If evangelists are to play their part efficiently they must be:

- Sure of what they want to say.
- Enthusiastic about their message. A teacher who is bored with the subject never inspires others.
- Sure of their audience. The evangelist must choose a style of presentation appropriate to the audience.

Interference in transmission

In personal communication a variety of interferences may be present.

- Physical interference: that is, the presence of other noise, such as that from traffic, children, or the television, which makes it difficult to talk.

- Metaphorical interference arising from the sender. If the evangelist is known to be a thief, immoral, or a liar, the message given will lack credibility. The lack of credibility may arise from much less obvious sins than these, however. In this case the old saying, "I cannot hear what you are saying because your life is shouting too loudly" can well apply.
- Mental interference. This arises when the sender has not thought carefully enough about the hearer. The evangelist may well be making all sorts of assumptions which are just not true, such as assuming that the other person has some Bible knowledge or an interest in going to heaven. The evangelist may be assuming that they have interests in common, which is a good basis for communication, but they may not have. The evangelist may be assuming they have a common world view, like a mutual hatred of evil or a middle class morality, which may not be true.

These will all distort the message as it is transmitted.

The decoder is the hearer

The hearers may not be able to correctly decode your message for a number of reasons. It may be that the hearers:

- Do not know what you are talking about.
- Hear, not what you said, but what they think you said.
- Automatically re-interpret what you say to mean something else, because of past teaching.
- Have been prejudiced against listening objectively.

Doesn't that make evangelism difficult?

We stated that communication is a complex business. Many of our problems arise because we take it for granted and do not think carefully enough about it. All evangelists ought to prepare thoroughly for their task. And yet, when you look carefully at what we have said, it all comes down to one thing: a question of relationships. Communication is about relationships and good communication demands good relationships.

It's no different from being in a family. Where relationships are good, family members probably spend a lot of time talking with each other and communicating is easy. But where relationships are bad they probably try to avoid communicating with each other and are probably very bad at it. They develop "selective deafness"; they deliberately misunderstand each other; they adopt literal and petty interpretations of what is said; they force people to say what they do not mean; they even shout at each other, but they still do not hear.

All evangelism, but person-to-person evangelism in particular, best takes place when a relationship has been established and where the evangelist knows his hearers well. *Finding Faith Today* (Bible Society 1992) underlined this very strongly. Most men come to faith through their wives or girlfriends. Other family members and friends were equally influential. Relationships matter!

USING THE BIBLE IN PERSON-TO-PERSON EVANGELISM

The advantages of using the Bible

If you use the Bible in your evangelism:

- It shows that what you are saying is not merely your own opin-ion and how what you are saying is related to God's message to human-kind.
- It helps you to focus on central issues, not peripheral matters.
- It will enable you to pin-point what you have been saying and bring it into high relief. A single sentence from the Bible can sum up in a memorable way.
- It can show how God is concerned about the complete range of human experience, even if your hearer's experience is different from you own.
- It firmly introduces the Holy Spirit into your conversation.

Before you use the Bible

Buy a small Bible or New Testament that can slip easily into your pocket or handbag. Get one you are comfortable with and familiar-ize yourself with it.
Read it regularly so you are well acquainted with its message.

Memorize parts of it carefully. This will give you confidence and authority in your evangelism. It is not as difficult to memorize things as most people fear. Think of all the facts we do pick up and learn quite naturally in the course of a day, or think of all the telephone numbers you know by heart. Of course the best way to memorize something is to use it. So it is with the Bible. Make a list of some verses which would be useful to you in speaking to others about Jesus and try learning them one at a time. When you have learned them, see if you can use them in conversation. It's good to make your own list of memory-verses, but here are some appropriate ones to get you started:

- Romans 3.23
- Romans 6.23
- Romans 5.8
- Ephesians 2.8, 9
- Acts 4.12
- John 5.24

Other references can be found in Chapter 3.

One of the good things about learning the Bible in this way is that it makes it easier to talk about it. If we really let the Bible become part of us we will almost certainly experience what Jeremiah discovered when he said, "But when I say, 'I will forget the LORD and no longer speak in his name,' then your message is like a fire burning deep within me. I try my best to hold it in, but can no longer keep it back" (Jeremiah 20.9).

USING THE BIBLE IN PERSONAL CONVERSATION

There are a number of things to bear in mind when using the Bible in the course of a conversation.

Introduce it wisely

A conversation is different from a sermon and it is unnatural to start a conversation with a text! Aggressive preaching at people on a one-to-one basis only brings conversations to an abrupt end. But in the course of a conversation the Bible can be introduced in a number of ways. You can say. "That's exactly what the Bible means when it says...", "Do you remember what Jesus said about that...", or, "I was just thinking that the Bible has something to say which is relevant...", or, "The Bible puts it this way...", or "I came across this in the Bible..." or perhaps, "God has said...".

Give it prominence

This doesn't mean you have to shout. But use the Bible in a way that stands out. It won't stand out if you use it too frequently, or if you are concerned with unnecessary details like quoting chapter and verse references; you need to know these, but they will probably mean little to the non-Christian. An evangelist doesn't have to be a verbal concordance. Introduce the Bible in your conversation at significant points, perhaps particularly towards the end of the conversation as a parting thought or when a crucial aspect of the Good News has been mentioned.

Quote it confidently

There really is no need to be apologetic about our use of the Bible. We delight in quoting public figures of today, or from the past, so why be shy about quoting the Bible? Being able to quote it confidently does depend on careful preparation beforehand and your willingness to memorize it. If, at first, you find your memory falters and the exact words do not come out, don't worry, just paraphrase the rest of the verse. The apostle Paul seems to have done that more than once.

Share it graciously

Never thrust a Bible into someone else's hand and tell them to look up Hosea 11.1. They will probably not know where it is and they may not even be very literate. It is good to actually produce a Bible from time to time and point to the verse or passage you are quoting. But if you do so, find the page yourself and then turn and stand shoulder-to-shoulder with your listener and point to the relevant words.

Handle it conscientiously

Remember what we said about the interference which destroys communication. In using the Bible we must be particularly alert to it. For example, don't assume a wide Bible knowledge. And don't assume that people will understand it just because you quote it. Try to get them to give you some indication of what they have heard you say in their own words. It may be helpful to ask, "How do you understand it?" or "Is that the way you see it too?"

Don't assume that people will accept its authority. Your listeners may mentally filter out all you say because they discount the authority of the Bible. You don't want to get into arguments about it, but you do want to bring such things out into the open and recognize them. There are three ways in which this can be done.

- You can hold the issue in suspense. For example, you could say, "Assume with me for the moment that the Bible is true and listen to what it says... That makes sense doesn't it?"
- You might want to meet some of the objections and so you might say, "I'm sorry you don't think much of the Bible; perhaps you can tell me why..." If they then offer a number of the common objections, such as that it is full of mistakes and inaccuracies, perhaps you could briefly point out the Bible's concern to accurately record the life of Jesus. You might also mention external evidence, such as the writings of Josephus and others, which support the Bible's central claims.
- Perhaps most effectively, you might put the ball firmly in your listener's court and say, "If you've decided the Bible is not to be believed, it means you must have been thinking about it. What would you say is the central message of the Bible?" This puts the onus on them to show whether they have understood its message before they rejected it. It also enables you to advance the conversation without being side-tracked from the central issue of the Good News.

Use it appropriately

Try to match the part of the Bible you use to the needs of the person you are speaking to. So, never harangue a bereaved person with harsh passages regarding judgement. Rather, be sensitive to their need. Psalms 8.16, 23, 30, 90, 121; John 11.17–27;

1 Thessalonians 4.13–18 and 1 Peter 1.39 are much more likely both to comfort and to communicate Christian truth.

There are psalms and parables to match almost every situation, besides the plain teaching of the Bible. And there will be opportunities for you to sit in their homes, or in a cafe, or on a train journey, when you can read the Bible to them. So, for example, consider the following:

The person you are speaking to is anxious — Psalm 46; Luke 11.5–13; Matthew 6.25–34; Philippians 4.4–7.

The person you are speaking to is a materialist — Psalm 73; Luke 12.16–21; Ecclesiastes 5.18–6.6, Matthew 6.25; 1 Timothy 6.7–10.

The persons you are speaking to are newly-weds — Psalm 37.3–7; Matthew 25.1–13; 1 Corinthians 13; Ephesians 5.21–33.

The person you are speaking to is resentful and unforgiving — Psalm 32; Luke 15.11–32; Matthew 6.9–15; Colossians 3.12–14.

These are just a few examples. There are many others which could be given. Why not draw up your own list of examples, bearing in mind people with whom you work or come into contact regularly. Note that some of these readings are quite short, just a few verses. Jesus was a specialist at packing in a whole wealth of meaning to a few sentences. Do not feel you have to quote the Bible at length for it to be effective. In fact, particularly when talking with the unchurched and those less familiar with books, it is just as well not to do so.

In our multi-cultural society it is worth asking if it is appropriate to use the Bible in talking with those of other faiths. The answer is yes. Many other faiths have great respect for their holy books and will treat your holy book with the same respect. Many will show this respect not just for the message of the book but for the book itself. So handle your Bible with care! A dog-eared, scruffy paperback, which might to you be a sign of good use, is likely to them to be a sign of disrespect. More comments on using the Bible in conversation with those of other faiths will be made later (see page 96). For the moment, however, note the advantage it may give you in witnessing, not to share your own ideas but to show the book is at the foundation of your faith.

Leave it prayerfully

If you can, carry some attractively produced biblical literature,
such as individual gospels or selected Bible passages, so that if the
person you are talking to is interested in the conversation, you can
leave them a copy. Your conversation may well have given them
an appetite to read it for themselves, and it can go on acting as a
silent evangelist long after you have left.

USING THE BIBLE IN PERSONAL CONTACT

It is possible to use the Bible even when little personal conversation has taken place, since it is quite capable of speaking for itself.
For example, a portion of biblical literature can be left in a home
where perhaps people are facing problems and decisions. You can
say, "I think you might find this worth reading. It will help you
with what you are facing at the moment." Often this is an effective
approach when visiting in a hospital. A patient may not be up to
much conversation, but having expressed your friendship and love,
try leaving a selection of Scripture for them to think about when
they are on their own. A number of publishers now produce very
attractive selections which can be used. You will find their names
and addresses at the back of this book.

Follow up

There are many other occasions when the opportunity to say much
about the gospel is limited, but when your "presence evangelism"
has opened the door for the Bible to do its own proclamation you
may find this opportunity at the times of transition we mentioned
in Chapter 2, for instance. Wherever a portion of the Bible is left it
ought to be gently followed-up later. Without interrogating, the
evangelist should provide an opportunity for those with whom the
literature was left to talk about what they have read and ask questions about its meaning. It may be that a simple question like, "Did
you look at that booklet I left?" will open up the conversation to
encourage them to look at it in the future if they have not already
done so.

Personal contact is preferable

Though the Bible can speak for itself, it is certainly better to leave it with someone with whom you have established some personal contact. There are many stories of people who have become Christians because of a Bible thoughtfully placed in a hotel room, hospital, or other institution. There are also a number of stories, and some of them are no doubt accurate, of people who have found a selection of Bible verses accidentally in the street or on a bus, and have become Christians as a result. But these are the exceptions. For every time such a result has been achieved we could speak of a thousand times when the literature has just been wasted or even despised. Leaving biblical literature around on public transport or in telephone boxes does not turn a person into an evangelist — it is more likely to turn them into a litter-lout.

USING THE BIBLE IN PERSONAL TESTIMONY

Your testimony is a brief account of your own Christian experience. Its value lies in the story being told in your own words and the way in which it shows God has dealt with one individual. It might be you can tell of a turning point in your life, when you responded to the Good News, or about the way you have always seemed to know God. People sometimes find it hard to identify with Bible characters or with the great saints of the past. But they find it easy to identify with someone they know and who has a lot in common with them. Ideally your account should contain three phases:

- Life before I met Jesus.
- How I met Jesus.
- Life since I met Jesus.

If possible, try to include examples which show how to deal with such problems as loneliness, and so on. If it is natural, it is good to include a verse or two from the Bible in your story. Don't look for them just for the sake of having them. But if God spoke to you through a particular verse or passage, or if there is one which exactly sums up what you want to say, then use it at the appropriate point. Again, use it in a way which makes it prominent. Don't bury it in the middle of a lot of personal details, which are probably unnecessary anyway. Don't fumble over chapter and verse reference. Put it in bold speech marks, metaphorically speaking, and let it carry its full authority with it.

8. USING THE BIBLE IN THE CHURCH

The church is probably not the best place to conduct evangelism these days. We have ceased to be a church-going nation and so most who attend will already be believers, although, as we shall see later, other people do turn up for special services. Even so, evangelism within church services still has a place for a number of reasons:

- The corporate worship of the church should itself be a powerful evangelistic tool. Paul recognized this in 1 Corinthians 14.24–25. The unbeliever coming into the church should react by saying, "Truly God is here among you!" The purpose of our meeting together is worship; the effect of our meeting together may well be evangelistic.
- Church services will attract a number who are interested in the Christian faith without being convinced of it or committed to it.
- The legacy of past Christian tradition means that people will still come to worship for special occasions. These may be personal, such as a family baptism or thanksgiving, or a major event in the church calendar, such as harvest, Christmas or Easter. Parents will often come to church when their children are involved in parade services, too. These can provide ideal evangelistic opportunities. *Finding Faith Today* demonstrated just how important such contact points were.

If we allow that church services do have a role in evangelism then we must examine what place the Bible has in those services.

THE PLACE OF THE BIBLE IN WORSHIP

Sadly, in many church services the Bible seems to have no cutting-edge. It is read in a predictable manner at a predictable point in the service, and prefaced and concluded by predictable sentences. It is often given less time than the church announcements. No wonder it fails to carry conviction. But this need not be so if we think creatively about its role.

Reading the Bible

Different church traditions suggest different forms of services and in some it is not possible to make many alterations. But wherever possible, consider the following:

- Choose the passage to be read carefully. Don't just read it because the lectionary says you must, whether it is relevant or not. Does it fit the theme of the service and does it relate to the sermon to be preached? This is even more important if there are second or third readings. Do they add to or illuminate the main theme? What is the purpose in reading them?
- Choose the passage with your evangelistic purpose in mind. Some will obviously be more relevant than others. Make it a special aim to introduce people to Jesus and choose passages from the gospels which show something of his life, work or teaching. Do this even if you are to preach from another part of Scripture, because most passages reveal in some way the importance of what Jesus did.
- Carefully consider the passage to be read. Where should you begin and where should you end? The paragraphs in the Bible you are using may not be the most appropriate, nor best express your purpose. Are there repetitions of detail in the parts you want to omit? What is the length of the chosen passage? Will it suit the attention span of the congregation?
- Always use good readers. If someone cannot read the lesson clearly and interestingly it is worth the risk of offending them by leaving them off the readers' list. The reading of the Word of God is one of the most important aspects of worship. It must be done well.
- Make sure that the reader prepares for the passage. Their role is to let its meaning be understood and they are unlikely to do this if they simply read it without prior preparation. The reader will need to know how the passage relates to the overall theme of the service or sermon and why it has been selected.
- Introduce it well. Long rambling introductions turn the congregation off before reading has started. But a succinct introduction draws attention to the importance of the reading and sets the scene, which enables people to understand it more easily.
- If it is a church where Bibles are provided in the pews, giving the page reference, the reader must bear in mind that in an evangelistic service there will be some people who will not

know their way around the Bible. So the reader should help them to find the reading without embarrassment, giving them time to do so before the reading commences. In such circumstances the passage should almost certainly be read from the version given in the pews.

• Conclude it well. Don't be predictable. Don't leave it in mid-air. Think of an appropriate sentence to say after the reading. But don't preach — that's the preacher's job later.

Dramatizing the Bible

One of the ways in which the Bible can be brought to life is to dramatize it in some way. Remember that much of the Bible is in fact a report of an event or conversation that once took place. Many of these are easily reconstructed. In this way even very familiar passages can make a fresh impact. Try the following three approaches.

A dramatic reading

Take Psalm 118 as an example. These are the words of a man going up to the Temple, telling the crowds of what God has done in his life. It also seems to have the occasional narrator's comment thrown in. So it is a psalm that can be read by more than one person at a time. We fail to capture its atmosphere when it is read by a single individual. It might go something like this:

Psalm 118

Narrator	Give thanks to the LORD, because he is good, and his love is eternal. Let the people of Israel say,
Crowd	His love is eternal.
Narrator	Let the priests of God say,
Crowd	His love is eternal.
Narrator	Let all who worship him say,
Crowd	His love is eternal
Individual	In my distress I called to the LORD; he answered me and set me free. The LORD is with me, I will not be afraid; what can anyone do to me?

It is the LORD who helps me,
and I will see my enemies defeated.

Narrator It is better to trust in the LORD
than to depend on man.
It is better to trust in the LORD
than to depend on human leaders.

Individual Many enemies were around me;
but I destroyed them by the power of the LORD!
They were round me on every side;
but I destroyed them by the power of the LORD!
They swarmed around me like bees,
but they burnt out as quickly as a fire among thorns;
by the power of the LORD I destroyed them.
I was fiercely attacked and was being defeated,
but the LORD helped me.
The LORD makes me powerful and strong;
he has saved me.

Narrator Listen to the glad shouts of victory in the tents of God's people:

Crowd The LORD's mighty power has done it!
His power has brought us victory —
his mighty power in battle!

Individual I will not die; instead, I will live
and proclaim what the LORD has done.
He has punished me severely,
but he has not let me die.
Open to me the gates of the Temple;
I will go in and give thanks to the LORD!

Narrator This is the gate of the LORD;
only the righteous can come in.

Individual I praise you, LORD, because you heard me,
because you have given me victory.

Narrator The stone which the builders rejected as worthless turned out to be the most important of all.
This was done by the LORD;
what a wonderful sight it is!
This is the day of the LORD's victory;

let us be happy, let us celebrate!

Crowd	Save us, LORD, save us!
	Give us success, O LORD!
	May God bless the one who comes in the name of the LORD!
	From the Temple of the LORD we bless you.
	The LORD is God; he has been good to us.
	With branches in your hands, start the festival and march round the altar.
Individual	You are my God, and I give you thanks:
	I will proclaim your greatness.
All	Give thanks to the LORD, because he is good, and his love is eternal.

There are many other passages which can be read in this way and many Bible conversations where more than one reader is helpful. The gospels are full of them. You do not need lots of resources of dramatic skills for this type of reading. You don't need great numbers of people either — four or five can make a convincing crowd in a church! Ask yourself if the readings you will be using on your next evangelistic service could be adapted in this way.

The Dramatised Bible published by The Bible Society and Marshall Pickering is a great resource if you want to use dramatized readings in your service.

A mimed reading

This is more difficult to do unless someone in the church is gifted in mime, but if they are it is a shame not to use their gift, as it an can be a brilliant means of communication. A passage can be mimed while it is being read. If so, you will require a good reader and careful practice to make sure that the words synchronize with the actions. But it need not be read at the same time as it is being mimed. To read it before or after is in effect to communicate it twice. In any case, the wider range of methods used to communicate, the more likely we are to communicate effectively. It is probably unwise to mime a Bible passage without reading it, since that assumes the congregation has enough knowledge of the Bible to enable it to interpret the mime.

Recently, a number of churches have been experimenting with

dance as a means of communication. It is an excellent and natural
way of expressing emotions and can evoke joy or sorrow. As a
result, when set against the reading or singing of Scripture, it lends
itself well to worship. Dance can be an extension of mime and so
may have a place in evangelism too, but it is a more ambiguous
means of communication and therefore has a more limited place in
this respect. Furthermore, most dance has a limited appeal to a particular culture, class, or generation, and so it may only be an effective means of communication to a small section of the congregation.

A dramatic sketch

The most ambitious method of communicating Scripture in an
evangelistic service is probably a dramatic sketch. If it is to be
done it needs to be done well. But it is not as far beyond the capa-
bilities of most congregations as people would like to think. Bible
Society's *Using the Bible in Drama* gives plenty of suggestions for
those who want to try and there are an increasing number of
resources to help beginners. The following basic points should be
kept in mind:

Choose a group. Choose them well in advance, so they can form
good, trusting, uninhibited relationships with each other. Good
relationships are fundamental to good drama. Give them plenty of
time together to pray, plan, and rehearse their contribution.

Choose a script. Are you going to use an existing script or write
your own? The parables are a good place to start if you are writing
your own. The advantage of writing your own is that the sketch
can be tailor made for the group and audience. But it demands
some skill and script writers should first be encouraged to study
Using the Bible in Drama.

Choose a style. Is the presentation going to be a straight reproduc-
tion of the Bible text in its original setting, or is it to be made more
contemporary? Much of the value of dramatizing the Bible lies in
putting it in a contemporary setting. The Good Samaritan is a safe
story until we remember that its equivalent today would involve a
minority immigrant group, a punk rocker, or even an IRA terrorist.
Only then do the feelings behind the parable begin to emerge. Old

stories can be seen in a fresh light if this is done. But it may not be appropriate to the congregation and such issues must be honestly faced. There is no value in shock if it alienates. But there is value in shock which draws the audience into the drama and helps people identify with particular characters.

Choose a place. This type of drama is by no means limited to the church. In schools, concerts, parties, arts festivals, and as a street theatre it has an even more important contribution to make. So even if it is used within the church, see if it can be adapted to meet other opportunities as well.

THE PLACE OF THE BIBLE IN EVANGELISTIC PREACHING

Preachers of evangelistic sermons cannot assume congregations will be interested in what they have to say, or have any background knowledge about the subject. It takes hard work to exploit the potential of the Bible in evangelistic preaching. The essence of such preaching is to make an identification between our contemporary circumstances and those in the Bible. It should be done in such a way as to make Jesus known and give an outline of the Good News. This should result in some response to Jesus Christ. How is this to be done?

Preparation

Preachers must think deeply about the message of the Bible and the situation of the audience (see the section on communication on p 61ff). They will need to read and re-read the passage from which they are to preach and ask what is happening in it and what truth God is conveying. It is important to start with the Bible and allow it to discipline the message, otherwise preachers may end up with only a few ideas of their own, rather than God's written word.

The audience

The preacher must think as deeply about the audience as the passage. It is a helpful idea to keep in mind a real but average non-

Christian and to ask how they could be persuaded about Jesus. Such an approach will discipline you to speak the audience's language, voice their objections, identify with their interests, and live in their world. Your preaching must relate to the real world of your congregation, and like it or not, for most that is the world of the TV serial, of major political events, of families and schools, and of major social problems. The preacher who can relate to last week's episode of a popular TV soap stands more chance of communicating than the preacher who has read a good quote from Tennyson in some book of quotations. Furthermore, our newspapers are full of contemporary illustrations and parables which will help us in communicating the gospel. This is also the point at which to decide whether or not you are going to use audio-visuals in your presentation. The preacher must think about all these things well before shaping any particular sermon.

Style

The evangelistic sermon must be full of conviction and confidence without being arrogant. It must aim to persuade; that is, the preacher must carry along the listener to the conclusion. It will be no good if the preacher talks down to the listener or denounces them. The preacher must be careful not to put the audience's back up because of the style of the sermon. The sermon must display a sympathy and understanding of people's circumstances. It must also be honest, raising real objections and giving convincing answers.

Introduction

I cannot think of a line more calculated to send a congregation to sleep than "My text tonight is...". Even if the preaching is to be thoroughly based on Scripture it must start with something with which the audience can easily identify. The preacher must earn the right to be listened to in the opening few sentences of the sermon. People will make quick judgements about whether to listen or not, as they do when deciding whether or not to watch some TV programme. So the sermon must deal with a felt need, or genuine concern. It could begin with a human interest story or build on a common interest. All these introductions can be found in the preaching of Jesus and his apostles.

Use current material

Such introductions are not hard to find. For example, one episode of the popular radio series *The Hitch-hiker's Guide to the Galaxy* begins with Ford Prefect in a pub ordering some drinks. He tips the barman handsomely because he says the world is about to end. The sheer incomprehension of the barman could be used as an illustration of the inability of many to believe that Jesus will return.

Peter Hain's arrest and subsequent protest that he had been wrongly identified some years back, would make a good starting point for a sermon on Paul's visit to Lystra, where he and Barnabas were mistaken for Greek gods.

An event like the Falklands War provided many individual stories which were useful sermon illustrations and a major illustration which can serve as a contrast to the message of the Good News. Britain and Argentina resumed peaceful relations, of sorts, but there was no reconciliation between them. What a contrast to the way in which God has dealt with his enemy, sinful humanity, according to Colossians 1.21–22. The strength of such an illustration lies in the fact that it is contemporary — stories about the Second World War now lack that edge and do not ring with the same note of credibility.

These examples show that the preacher must keep an eye open for stories in the news and listen for current topics of conversation. The more accurately the story can be told, and the more it strikes a general response among the congregation, the better.

In revising this book for its second edition, the author deliberately left the above illustrations in to demonstrate how quickly contemporary illustrations date. They were written just six or seven years previously but already have the feel of history. The Gulf War has superseded the Falklands War and the name of Peter Hain is no longer as well known as it was! The preacher needs to update his material regularly!

Content

The way the main content of the sermon is handled will depend on the passage of Scripture being used. With many of the narratives in the gospels and Acts the key issue is to create an identity between the contemporary listener and the original participants. Their two worlds must be bridged. It can be done by telling the same event in a contemporary setting or by drawing out the parallels between then and now. In order to do this careful research into the original background is essential and some of this must be shared with the congregation so they can understand the connection. But don't turn the sermon into a lecture. Wherever possible say something of your own rather than report what others have said.

Mark 13

In Mark 13, for example, the disciples boast to Jesus about the splendours of the Temple and Jesus tells them it is soon to be destroyed. Some information on when the Temple was completed, its size, the huge stones used in the construction of its walls, and contemporary opinion about it, all make it a real building rather than a cardboard cut-out. It makes it easier then to compare it to the splendid buildings of London which are the wonder of so many sightseers today. Just imagine if it was predicted that Westminster Abbey will come crashing down to the ground in a few years' time! From then on you can relate the worries and anxieties of the disciples about the future to our own insecurities about the future.

Acts 10

Or take Acts 10, where Peter goes to preach at the house of Cornelius. What an extraordinarily contemporary man he is. As a Non-commissioned Officer he would have had his full share of the experience of life. He was no "wet". Yet he was religious in outlook, generous in spirit, and prayful too. Like so many good, respectable people he thought he knew God, but how much more he had to discover!

Texts

Preaching from a text rather than a narrative highlights the next important characteristic of the sermon's content. It must be intelligible. Don't press texts into neat alliterative headings. Use plain ordinary language and make the outline fit the text. Using Romans

5.6–9, for example, we can preach on what the crucifixion says about:

- The condition of humanity.
- The gravity of sin.
- The love of God.

Or using Titus 2.11–14 we might speak of salvation:

- Why it's needed.
- What it means.
- How it works.
- Who it's for.

Or John 3.16, as drawing attention to:

- The love of God — for the world.
- The gift of God — his only son.
- The offer of God — eternal life.
- The condition of God — whoever believes.

Always make sure that the substance of the Good News is included. Of course, you cannot tell the whole story all the time — that is not expected and Jesus himself never did. But make sure that some of its major aspects, as outlined in Chapter 3 are included. And make sure that Jesus is at the heart of it. The trouble with a lot of evangelistic preaching is that it concentrates on trying to persuade people to believe without ever telling them what to believe, or rather who to believe. The existence and nature of God; the fact of mankind's sin; the facts and significance of the life, teaching, and death of Jesus all need to be taught today — we cannot presume that our congregation will know about them.

The gospels

Some years ago the New Testament scholar George Beasley-Murray wrote a helpful book called *Preaching the Gospel from the Gospels*. In it he reviews the life, miracles, teaching, and parables of Jesus and shows how each can be approached as the basis of evangelistic preaching. Many, for instance, find preaching on the miracles difficult. Part of the church wishes to spiritualize them and say that, though they never happened, they neatly express in concrete terms what Christ can mean to us. Some believe not only that they happened but that they still happen, and would find it an embarrassment to preach on them if that were not so. Beasley-

Murray, using the fruits of modern scholarship, insists that they must be taken as eyewitness accounts of what happened and then draws out why they are Good News for us today. They speak about the fact and the nature of the Lordship of Christ. They show the nature of his Lordship to be:

- The saviour of men and women.
- The master of evil powers.
- The Lord of creation.
- The revealer of God.
- The bestower of life.

Such a framework gives us a guide to preaching on the miracles of the gospels evangelistically.

Look at it another way. In Chapter 1 we made use of the Engel Scale (see p 8). Much of our evangelistic preaching is addressed to the levels minus 3 to minus 1 on that scale, whereas much more should be addressed in our present situation to the people who fall within the groups minus 8 to minus 4.

Quote

The preacher should quote the actual words of the Bible during his preaching as they carry greater authority than his own words.

Appeal

To be true to the New Testament there must be some element of appeal in our preaching. If an appeal is all it is, then it is unbalanced. But if an appeal is absent it is also unbalanced. It is not right for an appeal to be highly emotionally charged. Nor is it right to induce a false sense of guilt or psychological pressure in order to encourage someone to find relief. But it is proper to invite your congregation to choose. It matters whether people become followers of Jesus or not. Confront them with the choice, urge them to choose life and leave the rest to the Holy Spirit. If some of your hearers are to gain new life in Christ they will do so under the Spirit's direction, whether they display it in any particular outward way or not.

Earlier we pointed out that evangelism must be conducted at three levels — the levels of presence, proclamation, and persuasion. In a way these levels must be distinguished within the evangelistic sermon. The aspect of the presence emphasizes that the style of the sermon must be closely related to life now. The aspect of proclamation emphasizes that the content of the sermon must contain the truth about Jesus. The aspect of persuasion emphasizes that the aim of evangelistic preaching must be to persuade people to become disciples of Jesus.

EXERCISES

Here are some exercises for you to try. They will help you as you begin to talk about evangelistic preaching.

1. Examine Mark 5.1–20, Acts 4.1–22, and 1 Peter 2.24–25, then:
   - Draw out the parallels between features in the passages and our situation today.
   - List the aspects of the Good News included in each passage.
   - Think of a recent story or event which would make a suitable introduction.
   - Shape an outline structure for an evangelistic sermon on these passages.
   - What particular element of appeal would you use to conclude the sermon?

2. Try to turn the following passages of Scripture into dramatized readings:
   - Psalm 95
   - Isaiah 42
   - Luke 15.11–32
   - Luke 16.1–18
   - John 8.12–30
   - Philippians 2.1–18
   - Revelation 4.1–11

3. The New Testament preachers used familiar pictures from their contemporary world to illustrate the Good News of salvation. What scenes or events from our world would illustrate the meaning of:
   - Justification
   - Reconciliation
   - Redemption
   - Regeneration

4. The following brief stories recently appeared in the news.

- Decide how they could be used to introduce the Good News about Jesus.
- Decide what Bible passages they might illustrate or relate to.

Police recently raided a massive drug production plant in Mexico and freed nearly 8,000 people who had been forced to work as slaves.

Bishop Desmond Tutu has been awarded the Nobel Peace Prize.

A girl of 15, who had never spoken before because of a throat defect, spoke today for the first time with the aid of a new miracle voice box.

A father drove from Berkshire to Bristol and there threw his six-year-old daughter off the Clifton Suspension Bridge to her death because he loved her too much. He said he could not bear to see her grow up in such an evil world where she would be corrupted by drug pushers and sexual perverts.

Norman Tebbit was rescued after four hours from under tons of rubble following the Brighton bomb.

The Pope today visited in prison Mehmet Ali Agca, who eighteen months previously had tried to assassinate him, and offered him his pardon.

Egypt and Israel have signed a peace pact at the Camp David Summit. Hostilities between them are at an end and they promise peaceful co-operation for the future.

Man dies trying to rescue his baby son from a blazing house.

An MP has spent the week in a bed-sit in the north of England living on the minimum Social Security payment so that he could experience for himself the plight of the unemployed.

There was an uproar in a Stuttgart court this week when two ex-SS war criminals were set free. Former concentration camp victims stormed the judge's rostrum demanding justice.

5. Have you read or seen a recent:

- Novel
- Poem
- Film
- TV series or play

which could illustrate an aspect of the Good News of Jesus or people's reaction to that Good News? If so, how could you build an evangelistic talk around it?

9. USING THE BIBLE IN THE COMMUNITY

Paul was a man of one overwhelming ambition — to preach the Good News to people who had not already heard it (Romans 15.20). That is what makes an evangelist. As fewer people attend church it becomes even more imperative that we have the same ambition and take the Good News of Jesus to where people are, rather than where we would like them to be.

THE BIBLE IN THE OPEN AIR

Although preaching in the open air today is different to how it was in the days of John Wesley, it is still a viable means of spreading the Good News. Holiday resorts offer numerous suitable locations, as do market towns and other sites which traditionally permit free speech and amateur entertainment. The advent of pedestrian precincts and shopping areas provide further opportunities. Always obtain permission to use public areas from the police or council so that local bye-laws are not infringed.

Be sure to:

- Choose the site with care.
- Choose a place where people can naturally linger.
- Avoid causing an obstruction.

Usually there is no need for amplification, which can cause unnecessary interference or aggravation. The wise deployment of a small team can serve as an embryonic crowd which attracts others and draws them close enough to hear what is going on. A group singing or acting will also serve as a "pull". There are at least four ways in which the Bible can be used on such occasions.

In preaching

Preaching in the open air is not the same as preaching to a church congregation. It demands much more skill to hold the audience and one should reckon with the fact that many will only stay for part of the address or catch a snatch of it when they pass. This means that it should be:

- Short
- "Punchy" in style
- Avoiding a lengthy development of a logical theme
- Making use of repetition
- Quoting memorable words of Scripture
- Aiming to relate those words to a contemporary setting

With a sketch-board

Many have recently found value in erecting a large sketch-board and presenting the outline of the message visually as it is being spoken. This can either be done by the speakers themselves or by someone else while they are speaking. If the latter approach is adopted it should be carefully prepared together beforehand.

Pictures

Using the technique does not demand great skills as an artist. Attractive presentations can be made quite simply and for the most part it is a mistake to make them too complicated or try to include too much. Poster paint makes for a good bold presentation. Make sure they are big enough for the crowd to see.

Words

Words can be quickly and easily drawn by the use of ladder lettering. Draw what looks like a ladder lying on its side and then form letters by blanking out the appropriate part of the square with the dabs of paint. A little practice soon builds confidence with this. But to overcome any fears it is always possible to pencil in the area of each square to be blanked out so that no mistakes are made during the performance.

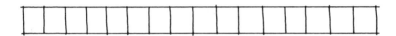

This is an ideal way of leaving the sayings of Jesus or other brief verses from the Bible clearly impressed on people's minds.

By using drama

Street theatre is an excellent medium for communicating the Bible. It is a crowd puller. Because the audience does not initially realize what it is watching, it removes any prejudices it may have about the Bible before they can take effect. It is a channel for communicating the Bible in contemporary language.

A whole range of Bible stories, parables, and events are suitable for use in this way. For more details see the previous chapter and the *Dramatised Bible* (Bible Society and Marshall Pickering).

Through distribution

Have suitable literature to distribute amongst the crowd or as people leave its fringes. This is an ideal way of helping the open-air message to remain with people long after the presentation has finished. Further, if an address is added, those who are interested can make contact if they wish to do so. When using an address choose a personal name rather than an impersonal institution. At the same time make it clear it is your church which you represent, so that you can be distinguished from the cults.

When distributing Scripture selections remember to:

- Smile and be polite
- Avoid argument
- Avoid litter
- Avoid making people in a hurry angry
- Avoid annoying people already over-laden with shopping
- Pursue any personal conversation that arises

THE BIBLE IN HOUSE-TO-HOUSE DISTRIBUTION

How to organize it

- Begin by praying about it.
- Choose a suitable Scripture selection or portion for distribution. It might be a selection appropriate to the time of year, such as Christmas, Easter, or Harvest. Or it might be a selection on a particular theme, or a whole gospel. (You can write to Bible Society for a wide range of Scripture portions and selections designed for distribution). Make sure the Scripture portion is in an appropriate language which, in some places, will not be English.
- Make sure all the distributors are familiar with its contents.
- Plan the distribution on a systematic basis so that no one is omitted and no one receives five copies! Consulting the Electoral Roll in the local library would be one way of obtaining the information you need.
- Train your distributors so they know what to do and what is expected of them.
- Team them up so they can visit in pairs. This means they can encourage each other and help out when one gets lost for words.
- Record sheets should be given to the distribution coordinator, and it should be agreed who will take up the opportunities in the "Notes" column.

WHICH STREET				
NO.	NAME	IN	LUKE	NOTES
1		✓	✓	
3		✗		
5		✓	✗	
7		✓	✓	shut-in
9	SINGH	✓	✗	Punjabi needed
11		✓	✓	Take S.School info

- Such work broadens the range of experience and can be a useful way of training the inexperienced. If it is an inter-church distribution programme it can be a clear demonstration of your unity.
- Work out a system of recording responses so that interesting contacts can be followed up. Judge this for yourself. If you ask if there is a need for a second item it should become obvious but if the house-holders say no then the door is shut for good. The visitor's card above could be used to help distributors keep a record of their visitors. If you decide to use something like this be sure to include a "How to use" session when training the distributors.

How to visit

- When the door is opened, smile.
- Introduce yourself confidently, stating the church from which you come, so you will not be mistaken for a sect or cult. People become defensive when answering their own door to strangers, so try to relax them and set their minds at rest. Make it clear you are not a doorstep salesman.

- Arouse curiosity, in a non-threatening way, by saying, "We were wondering if you had seen this?" as you show them the Scripture you are distributing.
- Follow that through with a brief word about the personal benefit you have received from reading the Bible.
- Stimulate their desire for the material. It will only be read if the person wants it. Try to show its local relevance by saying, for example, "You may have read about it in the local paper last week", or, "You may have seen a copy being given to some local personality in last week's paper". People are attracted to a product for a reason. People want insurance for protection, toothpaste to avoid dentists, and exotic holidays for the romance of the sun. Use the same approach in distributing the Bible. Motivate their desire by speaking of the way it deals with their felt needs for peace, love, freedom, forgiveness, and security.
- Listen to what is said in response. This will determine how you handle the rest of the conversation. Most will receive the literature politely and that will be the end of the matter. Some will reject it, in which case politely leave. Some will give the opportunity of talking further by mentioning a personal problem or interest, or by asking questions, or by raising objections to what you have said. Ask a few questions yourself to see whether there is any interest in taking the conversation further, but avoid prying and interrogation. Pursue the conversation as far as it will naturally go, then leave.

Some don'ts

Don't argue. Don't be defensive — accept criticism of the church but point out its value for you. Don't criticize someone else's church. Don't pry. Don't use religious jargon. Don't be sidetracked. Don't be dishonest — admit it when you don't know an answer. Don't carry piles of books with you — you'll get tired. Don't get discouraged — it's hard, but rewarding, work.

When to visit

Avoid meal times or times when most people are likely to be watching something special on the television. Never visit in the late evening and be particularly sensitive about visiting older people after dark. Visiting during the day will often reach a different group of people, so it's worth trying. Keep alert in case you call at an inconvenient time. Offer to call back at some more appropriate time.

After the distribution

Simply distributing Scripture portions without an adequate means of follow-up can be nothing more than a sop to salve our evangelistic consciences. Follow-up is essential. Follow up your visits with another distribution programme.

Another way of follow-up is to offer people to write in for further information or to offer the opportunity to attend a nearby discussion group to take the matter further. See below.

The Bible in evangelistic study groups

There is ample evidence today that one of the most effective methods of evangelism is the small study group. This is where a few Christians get down to looking at the Bible together with some non-Christians. It is a prime evangelistic method among students, but is just as useful outside student circles. Michael Wooderson's *Good News Down the Street* shows just how successful the approach can be in an ordinary parish.

There are a number of evangelistic approaches which can make use of the home as a base. A group can be invited to meet someone over dinner, or listen to an interesting speaker, or discuss a topical problem, or watch a Christian video. But there is no substitute for getting people to study the Bible for themselves.

The value of the study group

- People often find it more natural to visit someone's home than to go to church.
- A home provides a relaxed setting and therefore a good context for learning.
- A small discussion group allows everyone to take part on more or less equal terms, and is also non-threatening.
- It permits discussion at a much more relevant level than often

takes place in a larger group or the church. People can raise questions and voice doubts without being uncomfortable and can ensure they receive answers. The Christian cannot dodge the issue in this setting.

- It does not require the clergy to lead it.
- It builds relationships between Christians and non-Christians and makes caring for young Christians, if people are converted, much easier.

Starting a group

Pray. Plan the series you wish to offer. Ideally the series should last no longer than six weeks, with the option of dropping out after the first one. People don't want to get caught in an open-ended commitment. Few will refuse six weeks as being too much.

Plan the series around the events of the life of Jesus, which show who he is and why he came — passages like Mark 2.1–12 or Luke 13.10-17. Or plan around major themes about Jesus, which get the group looking at a number of verses and passages. The five topics Michael Wooderson has used are:

- Who Jesus was (for the first two sessions).
- What Jesus did.
- Jesus was raised from the dead.
- What it means to follow Jesus.
- Jesus offers eternal life.

Prepare the material using a modern translation of the New Testament and provide copies of it for use by all members of the group.

Training

Train leaders for the group and take them through the course them-selves. *Using the Bible in Small Groups* (Bible Society) would serve as a good training manual.

Invite those who are not Christians to attend. The place to start would be with church contacts. A personal visit or a letter followed by a visit to those who might be interested will soon elicit those who are. They should be given details of the course, so they know what they are letting themselves in for and how long it will last. Once they say they would like to join (and it is surprising how many will) arrangements can be made as to when and where to meet. It's not a bad idea to suggest that three people come to visit the house of the non-Christian, for if you are on their territory they are very much in control of what happens. The size of the group should ideally be between three and seven. Anything larger and the group will begin to behave differently.

Leading a group

Groups are not automatically successful. They need careful leadership if they are to work. The leader must not be a dictator, preacher, or know-all. The leader is there to facilitate a discussion, not to talk at people.

The leader must work at creating relationships. Even in a small group there will be individuals who need special attention. There will be the defensive, who need to be relaxed by a show of genuine personal interest; the silent, who need to be encouraged by the use of non-verbal signals like a smile or a raised eyebrow in their direction; the talkative, who need to be silenced by breaking eye-contact with them; the red-herring raisers, who need to be channelled by humour or gentle confrontation; the angry, who need to be wooed into participation, and so on.

The leader must develop the conversation. This is best done, after a brief introduction, by the right use of questions. Questions are least helpful when they invite the answer "yes" or "no" and when they are entirely open-ended, such as, "Does anyone have any comments to make on this?" The best sort of question is an open sort of question about a specific issue. These are the sort of questions which begin with "who", "why", "what", "where" and "how".

The leader must control the conversation to prevent it from becoming a monologue or dialogue, or from breaking into several small groups. The ideal discussion is one where every member of the group takes their part in speaking to every other member of the group. Rhetorical questions don't develop conversations. Throwing questions out to the whole group often gives only the most talkative a further opportunity to intervene. "What do the rest think about that?" or "What does anybody else say" are questions which include others in the discussion. Questions should only be directed straight at individuals where the group members have a great deal of confidence in each other.

The leader must direct the conversation. The study group should not be an open-ended meander; it must have a purpose. From discovery it must move through understanding to application. The leader must draw it all together and close it before it either breaks up naturally or causes people to be restless.

Building on the group

Towards the end of the series some opportunity should be given to those who want to respond to the Good News they have heard, to become disciples of Jesus. This can be done either at an individual level or by offering a special study which take matters further.

For those who have responded positively, it is important that they are now helped to use the Bible as the basis for their growth.

The Bible and ethnic minorities

The Bible is a universal book and has as much of a place in evangelizing those of a different cultural background as it does in evangelizing those brought up in the Christianized culture of the West. This is because many other faiths respect their own Scripture and Jesus as a great teacher. Nonetheless, certain things are very important when talking to people of other faiths. Your personal attitude is a crucial factor in determining the success of your witness. Prejudice, condescension, and lack of respect will destroy any potential there may be to talk about Jesus.

It is important to discover how much of the English language they know and obtain copies of the Scripture portion in their own language, if possible.

When visiting in an immigrant area find out all you can about their background, religion, and customs. Shape your evangelistic approach so as not to unnecessarily create barriers. For example, Asians have much respect for family, so it is unwise to permit unmarried couples to visit. Dress is important to the Asian and modesty is expected in women, so dress appropriately. They treat their holy books with respect, so do not mistreat any Scriptures you are carrying in their presence. Also remember that many cultures use their right hand to do good and important things, so try to give the gospel or selection with your right hand.

Avoid using terminology which will not convey your message. The word "Christian" is almost synonymous with being "British", so talk instead about being "a follower of Jesus Christ".

Accept gratefully any hospitality offered.

10. USING THE BIBLE TO GROW

The work of evangelism is not finished as soon as someone becomes a Christian. Few parents produce a child only to neglect it. Similarly, responsible evangelism continues to care well beyond the time when a person has turned to Christ. It aims to establish the new Christian as a continuing disciple of Jesus Christ and a member of his church.

God wants to see the new Christian develop and mature and is intimately involved in bringing this about. Paul said to the young Christians at Philippi, "And I am sure that God, who began this good work in you, will carry it on until it is finished on the Day of Christ Jesus" (Philippians 1.6). Peter was equally confident that "God's divine power has given us everything we need to live a truly religious life" (2 Peter 1.3). This does not mean that mature Christians can abdicate responsibility for the young Christian and leave it up to God. On the contrary, it means that mature Christians can be confident that they are working to fulfil God's purpose. They can also be sure that they are not working on their own, but that God's own resources are made available to them.

THE NEW TESTAMENT MODEL

Wherever new churches were planted in New Testament times the apostles were concerned to provide continuing care. Paul's letters were often written with this objective in mind. But contact was kept also through return visits or through messengers. Look at the study which follows. Work through it and see what you can learn about looking after new Christians.

Paul's example: A study in 1 Thessalonians 2.1–16

1. What motivated Paul's work? (Verses 4–6)
2. What pictures does Paul draw to describe his relationship with the Thessalonians? (Verses 7 and 11)
3. What characterized Paul's work? (Verse 8)

4. What aims did Paul have? (Verse 12)
5. What importance does Paul attach to the preaching of the Good News? (Verse 13)

The needs of the new Christian

Like any new-born child the young Christian needs:

• Love
• Nourishment
• Protection
• Training

These things enable the life which is there to continue to grow until it is self-supporting and can reproduce itself. If these needs are not met the life may soon fade away. A baby's needs are not just met, someone has to make an effort and a great deal of individual care and attention is necessary. It is the same with the new Christians. They need a mature Christian to establish a good personal relationship with them, and take an all-round interest in them, not just an interest in their spiritual progress.

It is because we have neglected these responsibilities that so many join the church and just as quickly leave it. Caring for new converts is essential to preserving the life which God has given.

THE PURPOSE OF CARING

In the long term the purpose is "to bring each one into God's presence as a mature individual in union with Christ" (Colossians 1.28). This can be reduced, in the short term, to a number of more specific aims.

To establish new life

In the very early days of Christian experience young Christians may well face many doubts, uncertainties, and questions. They may not be able to really grasp what has happened. The mature Christian must talk through all these things with them. Look at how Paul does this in 1 Thessalonians 1 and 2. Paul:

- Reminds them of what God has done for them (1.4).
- Goes over what they have done (1.9–10).
- Provides them with evidence so they can be sure of their new relationship (1.3–6).
- Encourages them to continue in the way they have begun (1.8).
- Answers the immediate questions (about suffering) which may cause instability (2.14–16).

To teach Christian truth

Too often we teach the mechanics of Christianity without ever teaching its beliefs. This is to put the cart before the horse. The Christian who knows what to believe will often practise what is right quite naturally. Recent converts will probably have little knowledge of Christian truth and we must not assume that they will find out unless we tell them. Here is a basic outline which concentrates on some of the great chapters of the Bible. This could be used as the basis for study. There are many other courses and outlines, some of which can be found in the Bibliography.

A BASIC OUTLINE

God

What he is like	Isaiah 40.12–31
What he requires	Exodus 20.1–17
What he promises	Jeremiah 31.15–34

People

Who they are	Genesis 1.26—2.25
Why they sin	Romans 7.7–25

Jesus

Who he is	Colossians 1.15–23
Why he died	Isaiah 52.13—53.12
What he does now	1 John 2.1–6

When he returns   1 Thessalonians 4.13–5.11

The Holy Spirit

Who he is   John 15.15–26
How he works   1 Corinthians 12.1–11
What he does   Galatians 5.22–25

The church

Ephesians 4.1–16

Christian living

Colossians 3.5—4.6

EXERCISE

Construct your own course for young Christians. As you do so answer the following questions:
1. What sort of person do you have in mind as you plan this course?
2. What syllabus would you plan?
3. What distinctive teaching, such as denominational emphasis, would you wish to include in your course?
4. How long would you intend your course to last?
5. What place have you given to the Bible in your course?

TO BUILD GODLY HABITS

Much early training consists of instilling regular habits into a child, like toilet training, washing, cleaning the teeth, eating, and even getting up! In spite of what some may say about habits, it is right that these become a part of our lives very early on; it saves us from much trouble later. In a similar way young Christians need to be taught good habits which will later enable them to live their Christian lives to the full. Such things should not be taught as the foundation of our life with God (see Colossians 2.6–19) but they should be taught as useful principles which enable God's life in us to be fully expressed. Four habits are worth emphasizing, Bible reading, prayer, church-going and telling others the Good News.

Bible reading

In reading the Bible we expose ourselves regularly to what God has said and build our relationship with him. It is a means by which we can "continue to grow in the grace and knowledge of our Lord and Saviour Jesus Christ" (2 Peter 3.18). Here are some practical comments about establishing the habit.

Finding Faith Today revealed that 91% of people who had recently come to faith said that the Bible played an important role in their faith. 62% said it was very important. The majority read it several times a week.

- Make sure the young Christian has a Bible which is readable.
- Set realistic standards about how much can be read profitably.
- Encourage it as a daily habit.
- Discuss the best time of day for it to be done.
- Introduce a Bible reading system or notes as a guide.
- Advise the young Christian to pray before reading.
- Ensure that the reading is thought about once completed.
- Suggest using the questions mentioned in Chapter 6.
- Talk about your own Bible reading habits and what Bible reading means to you,
- Share with each other what God has been saying to you through your regular Bible reading.
- Encourage each other to put what has been learned into practice.
- Recommend the habit of memorizing Bible verses.

Prayer

Just as any relationship develops through communication so our relationship with God develops through prayer. Prayer is not simply one-way conversation with God, but gives God the opportunity of communicating with us. So encourage listening as well as talking. There are a great many books on prayer which will help the young Christian. Find out about them and be sure to recommend them to any young Christian with whom you come into contact.

Church-going

Babies are born into families and Christians belong to the family of God. It is impossible to be true to God and ignore the church. "Though we are many, we are one body in union with Christ, and we are all joined to each other as different parts of one body" (Romans 12.5). The writer to the Hebrews rebuked those Christians who thought they could get along without the rest of the church (see Hebrews 10.25).

Yet for those without a church-going background it can be a difficult experience to join a church and they may well need all the help they can get. So make sure to offer them help to find and settle into a church.

Telling others

We have been thinking about using the Bible in evangelism and the young Christian is not exempt from the need to evangelize. Help them to be aware of this and use the insights from this book to help them to use the Bible in their evangelism.

TO PROVIDE AN EXAMPLE

Modelling themselves on someone else helps people to learn more easily than if they are being taught theory in a classroom. Paul knew this and often encouraged the churches he had founded to imitate him (2 Corinthians 4.16, 11.1; Philippians 3.17, 4.9; 1 Thessalonians 1.6; 2 Thessalonians 3.9). Like it or not, we still learn most by the example of others and we ought to recognize this in training young Christians. Rather than telling the young Christian to do the things outlined above we ought to do them with them. Since some of the issues may be fairly elementary to mature Christians it is important not to be condescending. Joining young Christians in doing the things that will help them to grow will only be effective if they can see the way we live and discipline our Christian lives. The best way to train involves forming a close relationship with the young Christian.

TO MOTIVATE CONTINUING GROWTH

This relationship must not be too close or else the young Christian will become unhealthily dependent on the older one. We aim for maturity and this means that young Christians must stand on their own feet and go on growing whatever happens to their teacher.

We can help to stimulate motivation by showing that we are still growing ourselves, or by talking of ways in which God wishes to become fully in control of the young Christian's life. It is then important to work through this with young Christians and give them the insights they need and support them as changes are made.

Start a group

There is much to be said for training new disciples in a small group. This was the pattern adopted by Jesus when he trained his twelve disciples and the inner core of three. The advantages of the group are that it:

- Enables them to learn from each other
- Enables them to stimulate each other
- Provides a natural support group
- Provides a wider range of experience as the basis for teaching and discussion
- Demonstrates the value of fellowship
- Creates deep relationships which can continue after the initial stages of discipleship training

If you need to start such a group, do talk it through with your church leader first. Make sure it fits into the overall scheme of the church and is known by everyone. Pray about it and then plan the course you intend to use. The type of course you choose should be determined by the aim you have in mind and the sorts of people who will be attending. Plan only a limited number of sessions to begin with, so that everyone can make a definite commitment to them. Think about how groups operate and study a book like *Using the Bible in Small Groups*. Be prepared for the demands it will make on your time outside group hours as relationships develop.

Once the group has started continue to pray and be patient. As every parent knows, growing is a long and painful process!

THE PLACE OF THE BIBLE IN GROWTH

The Bible plays a vital part in all the things we have thought about. It is not just that it provides the principles on which you should work, and is your basic teaching resource. The Bible is the agent of growth for the Christian.

The Bible gives life

The early Christians agreed that the Word of God, now enshrined in the Bible, was an agent that brought about new life in Christ. Peter wrote, "For through the living and eternal word of God you have been born again as the children of a parent who is immortal, not mortal. As the scripture says, 'All mankind are like grass, and all their glory is like wild flowers. The grass withers, and the flowers fall, but the word of the Lord remains for ever.' This word is the Good News that was proclaimed to you" (1 Peter 1.23–25). Paul believed the same, as we have seen from 1 Thessalonians 2.13.

The Bible gives growth

After the new birth, the Bible continues to be active as an agent of spiritual growth and change in our lives. So Peter, having said that the word of God was instrumental in their spiritual birth, urges his readers to go on making it their staple diet as Christians (1 Peter 2.2). Paul says that it continues to work in the lives of believers (1 Thessalonians 2.13). Hebrews 4.12 declares it to be a living word and active in urging Christians forward. James tells his readers that the most important thing they can do to be blessed by God is to "Submit to God and accept the word that he plants in your hearts, which is able to save you" (James 1.21). The fullness of salvation comes from putting into operation the word which God has made a part of us. John, in very similar terms, says that it is through obeying God's word that our love for God can be made perfect (1 John 2.6).

All this makes clear that the Bible is not an incidental if we wish to grow as Christians. It is the spiritual hormone that God has provided for our growth. It helps young Christians as they cope with the pressures of life. We cannot expect to grow if we neglect it or disobey it.

Multi-dimensional growth

The Bible is connected with various dimensions of Christian growth.

We read that it:

- Provides guidance   Psalm 119.205.
- Strengthens faith   Romans 10.17.
- Fosters maturity   Acts 20.32.
- Develops love   John 14.21.
- Overcomes evil   John 2.14.
- Increases confidence   Proverbs 22.17, 18.

There is no better summary of the matter than this one of Paul's

All Scripture is inspired by God and is useful for teaching the truth, rebuking error, correcting faults, and giving instructions for right living, so that the person who serves God may be fully qualified and equipped to do every kind of good deed.

(2 Timothy 3.16, 17)

BIBLIOGRAPHY

Resources from Bible Society

Bible Society has many resources to help you. We can supply you with: Bibles, New Testaments, Portions, Scriptures on cassette, filmstrips, slides, and many other things.

Write for a catalogue containing details of all our material to:
Bible Society
Stonehill Green
Westlea
Swindon
SN5 7DG

Evangelism today

The Logic of Evangelism by W. Abraham: Hodder & Stoughton
A Manual of Evangelism by C.Calver *et al* (eds): Marshall, Morgan and Scott
I Believe in Church Growth by E.Gibbs: Hodder & Stoughton
Evangelism, Now and Then by M.Green: IVP
How do Churches Grow? by R.Pointer: Marshalls
Good News to Share by G.Reid: Falcon
I Believe in Evangelism by D.Watson: Hodder & Stoughton
Evangelism through the Local Church by M.Green: Hodder & Stoughton
The Gospel Connection by M.Marshall: DLT
Finding Faith Today – How does it happen? by John Finney: Bible Society

Specialized aspects of evangelism

Preaching the Gospel from the Gospels by G.R. Beasley-Murray: Lutterworth Press
Time to Act by P.Burbridge & M.Watts: Hodder & Stoughton
Using the Bible in Groups by R.Hestenes: Bible Society
How Can I Turn the Tables in Witnessing?: Campus Crusade for Christ

Evangelism Explosion by J.Kennedy: Tyndale House, USA
How to Give Away your Faith by P.Little: IVP
Praise Him in the Dance by A.Long: Hodder & Stoughton
How to Begin an Evangelistic Bible Study by A.Lum: EVP, USA
Tell What God Has Done by R.Pointer: Bible Society
The Communication Process by T.Rowe: Epworth Press
Using the Bible in Drama by S & J.Stickley & J.Belben: Bible
Society
Parish Evangelism by R.Turnball: Mowbrays
A Guide to Preaching by R.E.O.White: Pickering and Inglis
Good News Down the Street by M.Wooderson: Grove Books

New Testament evangelism

The Apostolic Preaching and its Development by C.H.Dodd:
Hodder & Stoughton
Evangelism in the Early Church by M.Green: Hodder & Stoughton

The Bible and evangelism

The Bible in World Evangelism by A.M. Chirgwin: SCM
Attitudes to Bible, God and Church by J.Harrison: Bible Society

Introduction to Christianity

New Life, New Lifestyle by M. Green: Hodder & Stoughton
Knowing God Personally: Campus Crusade for Christ
New Life with Jesus Christ: Christian Publicity Organization
Basic Christianity by J.Stott: IVP
Journey into Life by N.Warren: Falcon

In addition, the organizations listed under Useful Addresses offer a
wide range of evangelistic and basic Christian study material.

Understanding the Bible

The Bible in Outline by J.Balchin and others: Scripture Union
The Bible: Fact or Fantasy by J.Drane: Lion Publishing

How to Read the Bible for All it's Worth by G.D.Fee & D.Stuart: Scripture Union
How to Read the Bible by J.Goldingay: Oliphants
Listening to the Bible by J.Martin: St Andrews Press
The Bible User's Manual by J.Balchin and Others: IVP & SU
Understanding the Bible by J.Stott: Scripture Union
User's Guide to the Bible by A.Reith: Lion Publishing

In addition several of the organizations listed under Useful Addresses offer daily Bible reading notes.

Basic Bible tools

Concordance to the Good News Bible: Bible Society
Cruden's Complete Concordance: Lutterworth Press
RSV Handy Concordance: Pickering and Inglis
The Lion Encyclopedia of the Bible: Lion Publishing
The Lion Handbook to the Bible: Lion Publishing
An Introduction to the Bible by John Drane: Lion
Modern Concordance of the New Testament: Darton, Longman and Todd
The NIV Complete Concordance: Hodder & Stoughton
Concise Dictionary of the Bible: Lutterworth Press
Black's Bible Dictionary: A & C.Black
The New Bible Dictionary: IVP
The Bible Commentary for Today edited by Howley, Bruce and Ellison: Pickering and Inglis
The New Bible Commentary (Revised) edited by Guthrie, Motyer, Stibbs and Wiseman: IVP
Peake's Commentary: Nelson
Black's New Testament Commentaries: A & C.Black
Cambridge Bible Commentaries: Cambridge University Press
The New Century Bible: Marshall, Morgan and Scott
SCM Pelican Commentaries: Pelican
Tyndale Commentaries: IVP

USEFUL ADDRESSES

Scripture distribution

Scripture Gift Mission
Radstock House
3 Eccleston Street
London SW1W 9LZ

The Gideons International
Western House
George Street
Lutterworth
Leicestershire
LE17 4EE

Evangelistic and Bible study material

Bible Reading Fellowship
Peter's Way
Sandy Lane West
Oxford
OX4 5HG

Agape
(formerly Campus Crusade for Christ)
4 Temple Row
Birmingham
West Midlands
B2 5HG

Christian Publicity Organisation
Ivy Arch Road
Worthing
W.Sussex
BN14 8BY

Inter-Varsity Press
38 De Montfort Street
Leicester
LE1 7GP

The Navigators
Tregaron House
27 High Street
New Malden
Surrey
KT3 4BY

Scripture Union
130 City Road
London
EC1V 2NJ